Praise for

How to Reinvent Yourself

by Marcellus B. Andersen

"How to Reinvent Yourself is more than just a 'how to' book; it is a powerful blueprint for personal renewal. I highly recommend this book to anyone wanting to make meaningful changes to their careers and their lives."

> —Dr. Lynda Falkenstein, President,
> Falkenstein Learning Corporation,
> author of *Don't Just Retire, Reformat!*

"If you would like to renew your life, you must read *How to Reinvent Yourself.* It's packed with common sense wisdom that's not very common!"

> —Ben Kubassek, author of
> *Succeed Without Burnout*

"This book is a powerful tool for self-awareness. The stimulating information contained in *How to Reinvent Yourself* will help you understand why you do the things you do, and more importantly, how to use this knowledge to bring about positive changes in your life."

> —Carolina Bont, author
> of *A New Reality*

"Marcellus Andersen's book, *How to Reinvent Yourself,* is an articulate and easy-to-understand presentation of many modern day concepts about how to transform your life. His focus on examining the beliefs behind one's behavior will allow readers to make meaningful changes. The stories from his personal experience and his obvious conviction about the subject make this book an interesting and powerful read."

> —Barry Neil Kaufman, Director,
> The Option Institute, author of
> *Happiness is a Choice*

What readers say about *How to Reinvent Yourself* . . .

"While reading this book, I often said to myself 'I never thought of it that way'—and what could be more valuable towards change than a fresh perspective? *How to Reinvent Yourself* provided me with very helpful ideas for improving my relationships, my career, and my life. In contrast to other books on the market, this book gave me concrete help and a new way to see myself."

—Tracey Erin Smith,
Assistant Manager

"I applaud your approach to humanity. We can only make the world a better place by first becoming better people ourselves. I have been inspired by your approach!"

—Coleen MacDonald,
Purchasing Agent

"An easy read! Andersen's clear thinking and common sense approach leads us to an understanding of our belief system. He shows how this belief system is a compass that directs our lives in so many different ways: how our mind works and perceives the world, the way we manage our careers and the manner in which we handle our relationships. This is a book I will be coming back to for frequent referral."

—Andre Bergevin,
Project Manager

"A remarkably clear account of how the mind can be put to work for you. This book is very useful to high school educators and counselors who wish to motivate students towards fulfilling their goals."

—Fabian Roberts,
High School Teacher

"*How to Reinvent Yourself* is presented in a concise, clear and simple manner. I emphasize 'simple' because many other self-help books are often convoluted and complicated, and the reader must spend more time attempting to understand what the author has written rather than implementing the suggestions. This book is a must addition to anyone's library."

—Yvonna D'Alessandro,
Actor

HOW TO RE·INVENT YOURSELF

Inspiring Strategies
For Personal Renewal

MARCELLUS B. ANDERSEN

Brooke
Press

Copyright © 1998 by Marcellus B. Andersen

Published by BrookePress, 2439 Eglinton Avenue East,
P.O. Box 277, Station A, Scarborough, ON, Canada M1K 5C1.

First BrookePress Edition, 1999

Cover Design: Marcy Rouske
Author Photograph: Faith Beilin

Canadian Cataloguing in Publication Data:

Andersen, Marcellus B., 1962-
    How to reinvent yourself: inspiring strategies for personal renewal

    Includes index.
    ISBN 0-9684682-0-9

    1. Self-actualization (Psychology) 2. Success. I. Title.

BF636.A53 1999   158.1   C98-901432-0

Although this publication is designed to provide accurate information in regard to
the subject matter covered, the publisher and the author assume no responsibility
for errors, inaccuracies, omissions, or any other inconsistency herein. Unless
otherwise indicated, all the characters in this book are fictitious. Any resemblance
to actual persons, living or dead, is purely coincidental.

This publication is meant as a source of valuable information for the reader,
however it is not meant as a replacement for direct expert assistance. If such level of
assistance is required, the services of a competent professional should be sought.

"Our deepest fear..." from A Return to Love by Marianne Williamson. Copyright
© 1992 by Marianne Williamson. Reprinted by permission of HarperCollins
Publishers, Inc.

Manufactured in Canada

10 9 8 7 6 5 4 3 2 1

*"It doesn't matter where you come from;
what matters is where you are going"*

Maxine Powell

ACKNOWLEDGMENTS

As I begin to go back in time and think about all the wonderful people who have supported me, encouraged me, and inspired me to write this book, I am filled with a profound sense of gratitude.

Gratitude towards my extraordinary wife, Faith, whose unwavering commitment to helping me make this book a reality resulted in her taking several months away from her own career to turn my sometimes muddy writing into a crystal-clear manuscript. Your contributions to this book, including your editing effort, your insightful stories, and many of the stimulating experiments, went beyond my wildest expectations and for that I'll be forever grateful. I couldn't have done it without you!

I also feel a profound sense of gratitude towards my mentors (those whom I've had the pleasure of meeting and those whose books I've had the pleasure of reading). Your revolutionizing work in the field of self-discovery and self-actualization has greatly benefited me in my own process of reinvention and has been the source of inspiration for many chapters in this book. I feel grateful to Dr. Wayne W. Dyer, for teaching me that we are much bigger than our limitations; to Ulysses S. Andersen, for showing me how powerful our minds can be and how to tap into this power by mastering our beliefs; and, above all, to Barry Neil Kaufman, whose pioneering programs on the power of unconditional love, nonjudgment, and the pursuit of happiness taught at The Option Institute in Massachusetts, have helped me create a richer and more fulfilling life experience. You are all in my heart!

I am also very grateful to Susan Williamson, for her editorial help; to Marcy Rouske for her great cover design; to Gary and Ann Ralston for generously contributing their time and business expertise; to Lynda Falkenstein for her invaluable publishing and marketing advice; to Auro Cellucci for contributing his ideas and experience on balancing work and home life; and last but not least to my family for their continuous encouragement and love.

Finally, I would like to acknowledge the helpful feedback from my test readers in the final phases of the manuscript: Coleen MacDonald, Dave Bergevin, Yvonna D'Alessandro, Nawdesh Uppal, Andre Bergevin, John Rosen, and Dave Gaudry.

This book is dedicated to my wife, Faith, whose love and support know no boundaries. Thank you for giving me the strength to make my dreams come true.

Contents

INTRODUCTION

The main goal of this book is to help you achieve success in your life—not only success that is measured in dollars and cents, but also the kind of success that is born out of personal fulfillment. This book will teach you how to develop the tools that will help you take your career, your relationships, and your overall life experience to the next level; a level where you have full control over the quality and direction of your life; a level where you have the freedom to make empowering choices, unhindered by fear or hesitation.

This isn't a book that tells you how to live your life, or one that gives you a "one-size-fits-all" recipe for change. Instead, it is a book that provides you with valuable insights into your own behaviors, so that you can identify and then remove the barriers that are holding you back on your path to success. As this book will show, it is our beliefs about ourselves and the world we live in that govern the actions we take in life. If we have beliefs that place limits on our potential, or beliefs that spell out rigid rules that we must meet before we can move forward, or beliefs that foster a lack of confidence in our abilities, then our actions will manifest in such a way so as to reflect these beliefs in our daily routine.

If we want to make lasting changes in our lives, we have to make our beliefs change along with us. This is what our process of reinvention is about.

How to Reinvent Yourself is a practical guide for helping you rewrite your beliefs so that they always work to your benefit. It provides an easy-to-follow process that allows you to identify the beliefs that are limiting your growth, release the hold they have on you, and finally replace them with beliefs that fully support your dreams and aspirations.

At the end of most chapters, you'll find experiments created to help you identify what *your* particular limiting beliefs are. Don't worry that you'll have to spend a lot of time doing homework, however. These experiments were designed so that they would only take a few short minutes of your time. In fact, you don't even have to do all of them the first time around, as any one experiment will provide valuable insights into your beliefs.

To make your experience more fulfilling as you read and practice the concepts and ideas presented in this book, I would like to offer the following suggestions:

- The concepts and ideas in this book build on each other. To fully appreciate a new concept, it's better to read all the preceding ones first. The most effective way of learning from this book is to first read it in sequence and then re-read any parts that you feel may help you the most.

- Be as gentle as you can with yourself when putting these ideas to the test, since it may take some practice to get good at them (getting down on ourselves when we "seem" to fail at achieving something consumes a great deal of the very energy we need to achieve it).

- To minimize this temptation, I have called the exercises in this book "experiments." The idea is not to pass or fail, but to try them out at your own pace. If you feel any resistance to doing a certain experiment, just skip it and come back to it later (there is a handy experiment index at the end of the book). Skipping is not an indication of failure, but simply that you are not quite ready to do the experiment yet. You'll know you are ready when you are naturally drawn to it.

- Finally, this book challenges many popular and traditional views that you may have grown to believe over time. As a result, I've tried as much as possible to refrain from forcing readers to take "leaps of faith." Instead, to the best of my ability, I strove to explain all the concepts with plain logic. Don't take what I say at face value, though. Accept it *only* if it makes sense to you.

Above all, have fun!

Marcellus B. Andersen

PART 1

REINVENTING YOUR MIND

*"The only thing standing between
us and our dreams is our beliefs"*

CHAPTER 1.1
OUR FIRST AND SECOND INVENTION

THE FIRST INVENTION

I have always been fascinated by how fast young children learn new skills and languages. What an eight-year-old can do after one summer of tennis instruction may take us adults two or three times as long to learn, or the proficiency a child gains after a couple of years of Spanish in grade school may take us several years of private lessons to develop ourselves.

When we were young, we could achieve a lot in a relatively short amount of time because we weren't hesitant or fearful in approaching our tasks. We went after every new experience with an equal amount of enthusiasm. We achieved most things effortlessly because our eager young minds were constantly open to them. When we tried to walk and then fell the first few times, we didn't give up. We didn't think "I'll never get it right" because we were naturally open to the possibility of walking. This natural openness gave us the confidence to try new things, however, it also left us vulnerable to the influences of our immediate environment.

The environment that had the most profound influence on us was the one in which we grew up. Throughout our upbringing, our parents trained our developing minds to help us stay out of danger. They brought us into this world with a lot of love and effort and they wanted to guarantee our survival by making sure that the "right stuff" went into our open and vulnerable minds, and the "wrong stuff" was kept out. During our school years, more right stuff was given to us by our teachers, and for those who had a religious upbringing yet more right stuff was handed down by our religious institutions. As we grew older, we started to be influenced in the so-called right direction by friends and relatives, and finally by our society.

Given our natural state of openness and our resulting vulnerability, it didn't take long for a lot of this right stuff to become deeply rooted in our minds and form a large portion of our early belief system. The majority of the rules, advice, and orders that were passed on to us by our childhood environment became part of our early psyches, mostly unquestioned.

At first glance, there is nothing wrong with the rules and advice that were conditioned into our young minds. Most aspects of our upbringing were positive and necessary for our well-being. For example, the importance of looking both ways before crossing the street is a good belief to impart in young children; or instilling empowering beliefs such as "If you fail at first, try again" can do wonders for the development of resourcefulness in a child. However, mixed into the medley of beliefs provided for our protection were all the limiting beliefs that our parents, teachers, friends, and relatives lived with themselves, in most cases unknowingly. As a result, most of us may carry today a number of beliefs that don't necessarily support the direction we want our lives to take.

Joyce, a woman in her thirties, recounted to me a traumatic experience from Grade 5 that she still remembers vividly. One day she had handed in her notebook to be corrected at the end of class. She was very proud of the innovative way that she had come up with to color-code her notebook according to subject material and day of the week. When she got the book back, however, the teacher had given her a failing mark because she "shouldn't" have used so many colors in the book. The teacher went on to ridicule the "mess of colors" in Joyce's notebook in front of her classmates as an example of what she didn't want to see from her students. Joyce felt crushed and embarrassed.

As a result of that exchange, Joyce began to develop the belief that being creative was unacceptable. Because her teacher had rigid beliefs about how notebooks should look, Joyce's initiative and originality were discouraged. While the teacher might have had good intentions in enforcing her rule about color in notebooks, the way she enforced this rule in the classroom resulted in hurting Joyce because it ridiculed her creative spirit. While one childhood event does not always result in the creation of a belief, it can certainly plant the seeds for its development if continually enforced. Interestingly, Joyce has told me that even now in her adult life she goes through a major struggle every time she tries to tap into her creativity.

When we are young, the comments of authority figures can have a profound effect on us, more than they might realize. Discouraging comments like those made in the above example can cause us to develop limiting beliefs early on in our lives. Even when those comments are given to us with the best of intentions, they can still result in the creation of insecurities and conflict in our minds.

For example, one day Ryan came home from school feeling very disappointed because he had received an unexpectedly low mark. His parents asked him why he was upset and he told them that he had worked very hard on an essay and was certain he would get an A for it, but was given a B instead. He felt strongly that he was robbed of the mark he deserved. His father reacted immediately: "Go talk to your teacher and get that A you deserve. Nobody should take away something you have a right to" (in other words, *Fight for your rights!*). However, later on his mother took him aside and advised, "Now, you don't want to offend your teacher by challenging his opinion. Maybe you deserved an A, but there's nothing you can do about it now. If you question his judgment, he may mark you down next time" (in other words, *Don't ruffle any feathers*).

While both parents sincerely wanted to help their son handle this situation, they ended up giving him conflicting messages. Ryan felt paralyzed as to what action to take because it seemed as if whatever he decided to do, he would be letting one of his parents down. While his parents certainly meant well in trying to help their son handle a disappointing grade, the beliefs that they taught him were opposite in nature, which resulted in a great deal of stress and confusion for Ryan.

The purpose of this chapter, however, is not to come up with reasons to blame somebody else for our present beliefs or to feel bad for being victimized by them, *but to become aware of the kinds of limitations that we may unknowingly be living with today.* Awareness is the first step towards change.

The beliefs that were passed on to us in our formative years, both limiting and empowering, are what I call our *First Invention*. Throughout this book, we will expose together any limiting beliefs that act as barriers to our progress and sense of fulfillment and we will learn how to effectively remove them from our lives. In addition, we will look at many empowering alternatives to instill in their place so that we can finally start going after what we truly want in our lives free of insecurities and self-doubt.

OUR SECOND INVENTION

Obviously, we didn't have much of a say in the way we were brought up the first time around, since we developed the ability to think and speak our thoughts only *as a result* of growing up. But now that we are in our adult lives, we have at last the opportunity to reassess our upbringing and give birth to our new selves. I call this rebirth our *Second Invention* because we are *reinventing* our beliefs so that they no longer place barriers to our progress, but instead provide us with unending support.

Before we begin our journey to our *Second Invention,* we need to be aware of three common traps that we tend to fall into when trying to make lasting changes in our lives:

Trap 1: It's common to think that we have to learn new skills in order to overcome a problem in life and move forward.

Fact 1: Before we can make lasting progress in our lives, we first have to *un*learn what is slowing us down. Surprisingly, doing this alone is often enough to solve our problem. Unlearning works so well because most of the problems we face in life are the result of learned self-imposed limitations (limiting beliefs) rather than the result of missing skills.

The concept of unlearning something in order to move forward in life may be difficult to accept, however, because we have been conditioned for so many years to believe that we can only achieve more by *learning* more. This approach may work to get a college degree or a pilot's license, but it doesn't necessarily work for improving the quality of our lives. How many people do you know who, in spite of learning new skills to improve their lives, or lose weight, or gain self-confidence and self-esteem, eventually revert in some way, or sometimes completely, back to their old selves? These people can't be expected to improve an aspect of their lives by just learning to use a new weapon, when their limiting beliefs are still in control of the army.

As we'll learn in the upcoming chapter entitled *Our Belief System*, our beliefs have a powerful influence over our emotions. If we have limiting beliefs, chances are that we will also experience limiting emotions. If we are trying to improve an area of our lives that challenges one or more of our limiting beliefs, the associated emotions will then kick in and sabotage our efforts. However, if we first unlearn those beliefs that place barriers on our path of growth, we will then be able to move forward unimpeded.

> *To make lasting changes in our lives, we first have to unlearn the beliefs that hold us back.*

Trap 2: It's common to blame the people or the circumstances that gave us the limiting beliefs which led to our setbacks and disappointments in life.

Fact 2: While identifying the source of our limiting beliefs is an important first step to understanding how we came to have them, blaming other people or circumstances will not help us get rid of these beliefs any faster. In fact, accusing others *slows our growth down considerably* because it keeps us focused on the past. Let's keep in mind that the people who raised us did the best they could given their own beliefs at the time.

To be able to reinvent ourselves, we need to realize that in order to move forward into our future, we first have to take responsibility for our present. Blaming others (or ourselves, for that matter) for our past will simply give us an excuse not to take this responsibility into our own hands, which in the end will delay our progress even further.

> *To move forward, we must take responsibility for our lives instead of falling into the temptation of blaming others.*

Trap 3: It's common to either ignore the existence of our limiting beliefs or to go to the other extreme and "declare war" on them.

Fact 3: Until we let go of our limiting beliefs, they will still have a great deal of influence over our emotions. If we declare war on them, they'll just use our own emotions to fight us back. If we deny that we have them and try to live our lives pretending that they don't exist, they may hide for a while and give us the impression that they won't interfere with our progress, but later on they will come back in a moment of vulnerability and sabotage some or all of the gains that we have achieved in their absence.

> *Letting go of our limiting beliefs has to be a gentle process. Shock therapy and denial do not work.*

Once we are able to unseat the first few limiting beliefs in our lives and replace them with empowering ones, we'll begin to feel the powerful impact of our *Second Invention*. When we are finally able to let go of a belief that has been stalling our growth for years, we will experience a profound sense of freedom. We'll be amazed at how much easier and faster we will achieve things that used to take us a lot of time and effort.

As we replace more and more limiting beliefs, we'll also be able to start learning new things naturally, not forcefully. We'll be able to reclaim the natural state of openness we enjoyed in our childhood which allowed us to go for what we wanted without fear or hesitation. But this time around we won't have the vulnerability of a child since *we* will now be in charge of what goes and doesn't go into our minds.

OUR JOURNEY OF REINVENTION

As we now get started on our personal reinvention, it's important to realize that our *Second Invention* is a journey or process; it's not an instantaneous fix. Just like it took time for our old beliefs to become ingrained in our minds throughout our *First Invention*, it will take time for us to reinvent them in our *Second Invention*. However, this will not take nearly as long as the first time around because *we* will now be in command of this process.

How much time do we need to invest in our *Second Invention*? That depends on the number of limiting beliefs we want to let go of, how deeply they have taken root into our belief system, and ultimately how committed we are to bringing about changes in our lives. But let me assure you: **this process will be the best investment of time you will ever make in your life!** It'll more than make up for the time you lose when you fail to take action because you *believe* you can't do it, or when you pass up an opportunity because you *believe* you don't deserve it, or when you get yourself down because you *believe* you are failing.

If you think you can't change because you have tried and failed in the past, or because you are too old and too set in your ways, or because of another hundred reasons, just think that you are the way you are **only** because of the beliefs you choose to hold onto. If you decide to take charge of reinventing your beliefs, then you will be on the way to living the life you truly want.

With these thoughts in mind, let's now embark on our journey of personal reinvention!

THE OPPOSITE RULES!

A good part of the limiting conditioning that we have received throughout our lives is based on popular rules and beliefs in our culture that we have carried, mostly unquestioned, from generation to generation. On the surface, they may appear to make sense, but in most cases they have little or no basis for truth. To be able to move past these limitations, we need to first expose them, then acknowledge them, and finally counter them with new concepts and ideas.

The Opposite Rules! is a summary of those new concepts and ideas as they are introduced in each chapter. You will find this section at the end of most chapters in the book.

POPULAR RULE		**OPPOSITE RULE**
To overcome a problem in our lives and move forward, we need to learn new skills.	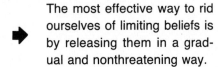	To overcome a problem in our lives and move forward, we first need to *un*learn what is slowing us down. Oftentimes, this alone will make our problem go away.
The best way to get rid of our limiting beliefs is by either "declaring war" on them, or by completely ignoring their presence (hoping that they'll go away).		The most effective way to rid ourselves of limiting beliefs is by releasing them in a gradual and nonthreatening way.

CHAPTER 1.2
HOW THE MIND WORKS

Our journey of reinvention begins with the mind, which is where beliefs are created and where they do their work. Ironically, the mind is one of the least understood aspects of our being. In ancient Egypt, when people in nobility died and were mummified, certain key organs were preserved separately in order to accompany the mummy's spirit to the afterlife. Among them were the heart, the stomach, the liver and the lungs. Interestingly, the brain was discarded because it wasn't given any significance at all!

Over the centuries, we have found it difficult to understand the power of the mind because it is based on the use of an intangible and indefinite kind of entity: the *thought*. In contrast, for example, to the concrete nature of our five senses, our thoughts remain abstract entities that are very difficult to trace. As a consequence, our modern society tends to focus the scientific study of the mind only on those aspects that are tangible and observable. The reality is that very little is still known about the true power of the mind.

But our lack of scientific understanding need not stop us from taking advantage of this great power in our everyday lives. In fact, we don't even need to know exactly what thoughts are made of and what they look like in order to harness the power of the mind. All we need to know is *what they can do* for us. And when it comes to doing, our thoughts truly have the ability to shape our lives!

Let's use a specific example to illustrate the power of thought in a person's life. A child is born into poverty, a situation that is obviously beyond his control. As a newborn, he doesn't truly experience poverty since he hasn't developed any thoughts on it yet. In his early life, this child will not know that he is poor, since he doesn't really have any point of reference for comparison. As far as this young child is concerned, he's neither poor nor rich; *he simply is*.

During this early time of his life, his only thoughts will center around being fed when his little body tells him of this need and feeling satisfied once he's been fed (no different than a newborn raised in a wealthy household). However, as the child grows up, he begins to be told by his environment that he is poor, and also what being poor means and will mean throughout his life. Moreover, the media will provide him with ample information about what being rich is like, so the child will now be able to compare the so-called poor lifestyle he has versus the material abundance "others" have.

All of this conditioning will generate thoughts of poverty into his mind. *It is only when these thoughts take root that he will truly become poor. And he will remain so as long as he retains these thoughts in his mind.* The good news is that the limiting thoughts that have resulted in this child's experience of poverty aren't permanent and can be replaced by new thoughts of prosperity. These new thoughts have in turn the potential for completely transforming this child's experience into one of wealth and abundance, in spite of his present circumstances.

A story comes to mind about a physician in Washington D.C. who called into a radio talk show where author Dr. Wayne W. Dyer was being interviewed about this very subject. The caller related that he had been raised in dirt-poor conditions, but as a child he had always had a vision of himself as a doctor. When he got older and finished high school, he applied to several hundred pre-med schools and was rejected over and over again. But he refused to let go of his vision and eventually his persistence paid off when one pre-med school gave him a conditional opportunity to enroll. Many years later, at the time of calling into the radio talk show, his vision had become a reality and he now enjoyed a thriving medical practice. Interestingly, he also related that most of his brothers and sisters still lived in the same conditions of poverty in which he had been raised.

This man was born into extreme poverty, a circumstance he obviously didn't choose. But he refused to let this circumstance determine his fate and instead decided to foster the thought that one day he would become a doctor. He applied so much conviction to this thought that it became a very empowering belief. In fact, so powerful was this belief that it gave him the strength to persist in the face of hundreds of rejection letters, until he finally received the one letter of acceptance that launched his dream. If he had allowed himself to become a victim of his circumstances, he would have given up after the first few rejections. For instance, he might have thought: "Who am I anyway living in such poor conditions to even think about going to medical school?"

In the end, the difference between being accepted into medical school and remaining a victim of his present circumstances really boiled down to a *thought applied with a lot of conviction*. Neither the rejection by hundreds of schools nor the dirt-poor conditions in which he was born were able to stop this man from achieving his dream. **His relentless thought of becoming a doctor created a powerful belief which ultimately turned his life around from an experience of lack to one of prosperity.**

By birthright, we <u>all</u> have the ability to harness the power of our thoughts. We just have to learn how to tap into this power effectively so that we can bring about positive changes in our own lives. How do we go about doing this? We can begin by learning from those people who are constantly expanding the reaches of their own potential, through creating something that has never existed before or achieving something that was never previously thought possible. When these people are asked about the secret of their success, they invariably give some version of the following answer:

To succeed in doing something you've never attempted before, you must first have the belief that it can be done.

As an example, I once read about an interview with Thomas Edison that took place right after his celebrated invention of the electric light bulb, which, incidentally, took him 10,000 trials to get to work. The interviewer asked him what it was that made him persist until the very end, when most people would have given up after only several dozen trials, or maybe a couple hundred trials, let alone 10,000! Edison answered that he always believed that the electric light bulb invention was possible and that it was just a matter of time before somebody would get it right. "Besides," he said, "after so many failures I knew that one day I would eventually run out of ways for the light bulb not to work."

As proven by the physician from Washington D.C., Thomas Edison, countless athletes, and many other high achievers in our society, before a desired reality manifests for us, we need to have it strongly present in our minds. Sometimes this is achieved consciously, sometimes subconsciously. **But in either case, we'll find that our beliefs have played a significant role in the process.**

THE CONSCIOUS AND SUBCONSCIOUS MIND

The first step toward taking full advantage of the "secret of success" high achievers talk about, is to have a basic understanding of how the mind works and how our beliefs operate within it.

Our minds have a dual nature: a *conscious mind* and a *subconscious mind*. The conscious mind houses our *logic*, *reason*, and *thinking*. This is the part of the mind that provides control in our lives. It receives input from our five senses and then uses this information to help us perform all the everyday tasks necessary for our existence. Our conscious mind triggers us to look for food when we are hungry, to search the want ads when we are looking for a job, or to go to the bank when our wallet is empty. The conscious mind is devoid of emotions, creativity, or imagination. It is simply designed to fulfill its primary job of helping us provide for and protect ourselves.

When we are born, our conscious mind is undeveloped. As a newborn, our mind doesn't possess any logic or reason. If we are hungry, all we can do is cry out of our discomfort. We are not yet equipped with the logic necessary to look for food ourselves. If nobody responds to our call for help, we will starve to death. We depend completely on others for our protection, since our own protection mechanism, the conscious mind, has not yet evolved.

As we grow up, we start depending on others less and less because, along with our growing body, our conscious mind is beginning to develop the intellectual capacity required to function without external help. Adulthood typically denotes the point in the development of our conscious mind where we have become self-sufficient.

The subconscious mind, on the other hand, houses our *creativity, imagination*, and *beliefs*. It is devoid of logic and reason, and therefore has no controlling mechanism of its own. The subconscious mind relies almost entirely on the conscious mind as its primary source of control.

When we are born, our subconscious mind is well in place even when our conscious mind is in the early stages of development. The subconscious mind provides the unending source of vivid imagination and fantasy that children possess. It is also the source of our dreams. Very young children, for example, are known to dream well before they show any signs of intellectual thought or logic.

The subconscious is the part of our mind that never sleeps. While our conscious mind shuts down for the day, our subconscious mind is very busy in our sleep. Our dreams are an indication of the activities of our working subconscious mind uncensored by our resting logical conscious mind. This explains, for instance, why we can have extremely realistic dreams in which we are performing feats that are impossible in the eyes of our conscious mind, such as falling off a cliff and halfway down realizing that we can actually fly; or willing a gourmet feast, and then having it appear instantaneously in front of our delighted faces.

HOW THOUGHTS BECOME BELIEFS

Let's now look at how our beliefs function in the context of our conscious and subconscious mind. On any given day there are hundreds of thoughts crossing our minds. Since thinking is a conscious process, one of the jobs of our conscious mind is to screen our thoughts and single out those that are useful for our protection and well-being. Once a thought has been selected, our conscious mind then passes it along to the subconscious mind where it is registered as an experience for future reference.

If the selected thought carries sufficient conviction, however, the subconscious mind will turn it into a belief. Alternatively, if this thought doesn't carry enough conviction the first time around but is re-sent to our subconscious mind repeatedly over a period of time, it might still be turned into a belief, since each time a thought is re-sent its level of conviction increases (which is commonly referred to as *conditioning*). From this point onward, our behavior and our actions will be adjusted automatically to reflect this new belief.

Thoughts applied with
conviction turn into beliefs.

Let's illustrate the creation of beliefs with an example. Let's say that we have an idea for a product or service and decide to start a small business. We are excited about it and also a bit nervous since we have never done this kind of thing before. Due to our lack of experience, however, we don't plan it very well and as a result our first business deal falls through.

One of two things may happen now. First scenario: if we see this experience as a failure and get really down on ourselves, our conscious mind will protectively pass a thought to our subconscious mind acknowledging the negative experience for future reference.

This thought may not carry enough conviction yet to be turned into a belief. But if the next couple of deals also fall through, the repetition of this experience of failure may condition our subconscious mind with the thought that "No matter how hard I try, I can't make a go at having my own small business." If this thought is conditioned a number of times, enough conviction will be generated to ingrain it deeply in our subconscious.

Once this has taken place, we'll have a new limiting belief in our belief system that will almost certainly discourage us from attempting to start a small business in the future.

In essence, our conscious mind is performing its primary job of protecting us: if every time a deal falls through we suffer from frustration and anger, it will pass enough information to the subconscious mind to create a belief that *will stop us from taking any action that would make us endure this pain again in the future*. It doesn't matter to the conscious mind whether the resulting belief is limiting or empowering for us; what matters is that we *must* be protected from the pain we experience every time we fail.

As far as the subconscious mind is concerned, it cannot stop the creation of this belief since it has no controlling mechanism of its own. Remember that the conscious mind controls its input. The subconscious mind always assumes that whatever the conscious mind sends its way is necessary for our protection.

Now, not all beliefs required for our protection are limiting. For instance, let's now consider a second scenario for our business venture. Let's say that this time, instead of getting ourselves down when we fail, we have the attitude that this is not really a failure but a learning experience. In this case, since our well-being is not being threatened, our conscious mind will <u>not</u> pass a protective thought to our subconscious mind. Because we have the attitude that this is not a failure, but is instead a learning experience, we will have our confidence intact to make new attempts unhindered by fear and hesitation.

The good news is that if we manage to keep up this positive attitude until we succeed (which is now more feasible since our energy is focused on learning and not on blaming ourselves), then an empowering belief will be created instead in our subconscious mind: "I can succeed at any business venture that I start."

What a difference with the belief created in the first scenario! Our conscious mind is still fulfilling its role of protecting our well-being, but this time it's ingraining *empowering* thoughts into our subconscious mind which will create a belief that supports us the next time we are faced with a similar challenge. These two scenarios, based on the very same facts, resulted in two completely opposite experiences for us.

What is it, then, that makes us respond one way or another? Why do some people respond by getting themselves down and some others by having a more hopeful and positive attitude?

BELIEFS FROM OUR UPBRINGING

The answer lies in the beliefs that we were conditioned with throughout our upbringing. While some of us were always encouraged to try again whenever we failed, some of us were pressured to be perfect the first time around, so when we came short of that ideal we automatically got down on ourselves. Interestingly, it is these beliefs from our upbringing that are the most influential on our behavior as adults because they are so deeply imbedded in our psyches. The deeper a belief is ingrained into our subconscious, the more influence it has on our behavior.

Beliefs developed during childhood still exert a significant influence over our behavior as adults.

Let's explain why this happens in terms of our conscious and subconscious mind. As stated before, when we are born our conscious mind is undeveloped, but our subconscious mind is already in place. As a result, we don't yet have the protective shield of the conscious mind to filter what goes or doesn't go into our subconscious, even though our subconscious mind is fully capable of creating beliefs.

The fact that we didn't have this protective shield when we were young made us very vulnerable because it left a direct path open from the environment to our subconscious. If somebody in our immediate environment gave us advice, asserted a rule, or punished us for something we did, and they did it with enough conviction, then our subconscious mind turned this advice, rule, or punishment into a belief. The stronger the conviction that was used, the deeper the belief was ingrained, and the more influence this limiting or empowering belief now has on our behavior.

For example, Jessica was brought up with the belief that "Only perfect practice makes perfect." Through the attitudes and words of her parents, she was made to understand that what she did wouldn't be good enough unless it was perfect from the word go. As a result, she grew up with the belief that there was no point in trying anything unless she could do it perfectly the first time around. To reinforce this belief even further in her young mind, whenever she tried something for the first time and failed at it, she was lectured by her parents for not having tried "hard enough."

Now, in her adult life, Jessica feels a lot of resistance any time she wants to attempt something new. As soon as she makes up her mind to do something different, thoughts from the past start flooding her mind: "If I can't do it perfectly, there's no point in trying at all," "If I can't succeed right away, why bother?" Even when she actually gets the courage to make an attempt, but doesn't succeed initially, she gives up and justifies it to herself by saying "What's the point in trying again? If I can't be perfect the first time, then I'll never be perfect."

If, on the other hand, Jessica had grown up with "If you fail at first, try again" and had been encouraged by her parents to do so whenever she didn't "get it right," she would have had a completely different experience. Therefore, her response as an adult would also be totally different. In trying something new and failing the first time, Jessica might look at the experience and say, "That's too bad it didn't go as I planned, but let's see what I have to learn from this.

And I had fun doing it anyway, so I want to try it again!" This belief helps her create a more fulfilling life because it isn't based on an unattainable level of perfection, but instead on learning from mistakes in order to improve oneself.

It is this kind of conditioning from our upbringing that can place us in the "I'll never try again" scenario or the "Let's learn from our mistakes and move on" scenario of our earlier business example. If we carry limiting beliefs about failure with us, chances are we'll fall into the first scenario and get ourselves down for our apparent "blunder." If instead we carry empowering beliefs about failure with us, chances are we'll fall into the second scenario and see each new attempt as a learning experience.

Let's keep in mind, however, that whether we fall into the first or second scenario is not primarily decided on a conscious level. Our present beliefs will *subconsciously* influence our behavior. It's highly unlikely that we'll stop after the first business failure to ask ourselves: "Am I going to beat myself up for this failure or am I going to learn from this experience?" The behavior that we exercise will more likely be an automatic reflection of our beliefs.

But just because we have been conditioned with certain beliefs, doesn't mean that we cannot change them. At this point, however, it's enough to know that they exist and not to concern ourselves with replacing them just yet. In this early stage of our process of reinvention, we are becoming aware of those beliefs that limit our potential so that we can eventually replace them with ones that can support us. Starting with the next chapter, we'll begin focusing on more specific aspects of our lives in which the reinvention of our beliefs can make a significant contribution to our personal growth.

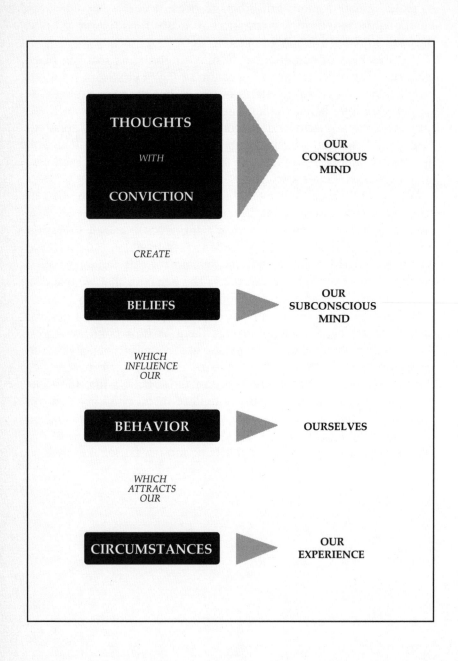

THE OPPOSITE RULES!

POPULAR RULE	**OPPOSITE RULE**
We have no control over our circumstances.	We can **attract** any circumstances we want just by changing our beliefs.

The diagram to the left summarizes the process of creation of our beliefs, how they influence our behavior, and how they ultimately define our experience. We can see that thoughts applied with conviction by the conscious mind turn into beliefs in the subconscious mind. These beliefs influence our behavior (which characterizes who we are), and ultimately, our behavior attracts our circumstances (the experience we call our lives).

EXPERIMENT:
IDENTIFYING COMMON LIMITING BELIEFS

In this experiment, simply look over the following list of common limiting beliefs and check any of the ones you feel apply to you. Don't concern yourself with how many you identify with or how you'll get rid of them. That comes later. The first step is to become aware of what they are.

- I never have enough money.

- I'm too young to succeed.

- I'm too old to change jobs.

- If I can't be perfect, I won't even try.

- To be loved, I have to be a victim.

- If I succeed, people won't like me.

- If I succeed, something bad will happen.

- I don't have what it takes to succeed.

- I can never make ends meet.

- If I do well this time, I must always do well.

- If I'm not successful, I am nothing.

- If life is going too good, something has to be wrong.

- If I didn't go to college, I can't be successful.

- I can't change because I've tried and failed before.

- I'll never attain my ideal weight.

- Even if I can lose weight, I won't be able to keep it off.

- I can't survive on my own.

- I'm too old to make a difference.

Chapter 1.3
Our Belief System

O ur belief system is the collection of all the beliefs that we have inherited and developed throughout our lives, whether they are empowering or limiting, positive or negative, effective or ineffective. All of them touch our lives in very powerful ways. Let's now take an in-depth look at how our belief system influences our everyday experience; more specifically: how it influences the way we *see* the world around us, the way we *feel* about the world we see, and the way we *behave* as a result.

Our Beliefs and Our Reality

Of all the timeless expressions that have been passed on from generation to generation, one of the most popular ones around is "I have to see it to believe it." For ages, this expression has served as the basis for defining our everyday reality. Essentially, it means that we'll accept an event as real only if it has registered with our senses; in other words, we make our senses the objective judge of our experience. But how objective can our senses really be?

One evening I was fixing dinner at home and I wanted to use the salt shaker. I usually keep it in the third cupboard to the left of the refrigerator. But when I went to look for it, I couldn't find it. I asked my wife, who was reading in the living room, if she had used it or seen it lately. She said that she had used it for lunch but had put it back.

I checked the third cupboard again in case I missed it the first time and it wasn't there. Then, I opened all of the doors, but still couldn't find it. In frustration, I asked my wife to come over and help me find that darn salt shaker. She came into the kitchen, walked directly to one of the open doors and grabbed it right out from under my nose! Has something like this ever happened to you?

The selective "blindness" I experienced is just one example of the subjective nature of our reality. Essentially, what we deem as real isn't based on what comes through our senses, but is instead based on the images that register in our minds <u>after</u> being filtered by our beliefs. What we see and what gets imprinted into our minds are two separate things. At some point my eyes *looked* right at the salt shaker, but because I didn't believe I would find it where I saw it, my belief system edited it out of my field of vision. In the end, I didn't see the salt shaker because I didn't *believe* I would find it any place other than where I have always left it (behind the third door). This is an example of how our minds can alter our view of the world in order to conform to our beliefs. It seems that the old adage "I have to see it to believe it" should be rewritten more appropriately to "I have to believe it in order to see it."

What the salt shaker example also demonstrates is that different people can experience a different reality even when witnessing the same event. Sometimes they might even be standing in front of the same object, and yet have totally different experiences. For instance, let's say that two people are looking at a baseball bat. However, the first person sees it as a fun piece of sports equipment that brings back a lot of good memories from childhood, while the second person sees it as a blunt object of violence similar to the one that was used to brutally beat him in a gang attack a few years earlier. The beliefs these two people hold about baseball bats will ultimately create two very different realities for them, even though the object they are both looking at (the baseball bat) is the same.

The fact that we always see our own individual reality based on what our beliefs are carries powerful benefits. While the world around us may not always be under our control, *our beliefs about it are*. As a result, we can learn to reshape our reality through changing our beliefs so that it continuously works for us and not against us.

OUR BELIEFS AND OUR EMOTIONS

Given that our beliefs influence the way we *see* things in life, let's now look at how they influence the way we *feel* about what we see.

Let's say a friend stands you up. How does that make you feel? Mildly annoyed? Angry? Incensed? When someone stands me up, I actually feel confused because I am not sure if I misunderstood the time or place we were supposed to meet. My wife gets upset instead because she has a high regard for consideration and she feels that standing someone up is highly inconsiderate. A dear friend of mine once told me that one day back in college he had arranged to meet a classmate at 3 PM. He was running late and showed up quite embarrassed at 4:30 PM, a full hour and a half past the agreed time. His friend showed up five minutes later! They started laughing hysterically.

Whenever we react to a given situation, we automatically assume that the situation itself is the cause of our reaction. After all, it's the highway ramp that was unexpectedly closed that ruined our commute home as well as our evening, or the woman who double-charged us for an item at the checkout counter who ripped us off.

But if the situations were the true cause of our reactions, then why doesn't everybody respond in exactly the same way to the same situation? If this logic is indeed true, then my friend, my wife, and myself should all have reacted in the same way to being stood up.

However, depending on the individual, there is a whole gamut of responses to any given situation ranging anywhere from anger to confusion to simple and enjoyable laughter. Obviously, there must be something independent of the situation that triggers our emotions. Since each one of us experiences a different reality based on our beliefs at the time, then the way we feel about what we witness must also be different for everyone. **The reason people react differently to the same situation is that each person's beliefs about it are different.** The situation itself is *not* the true source of our emotions; our beliefs are.

To use the highway example above: our evening is not ruined because of a closed down stretch of asphalt and cement, but because of our beliefs about what the closed highway means to us. Some people may blame themselves because they heard about the ramp closure and forgot about it and they believe that self-blame is the punishment they deserve for not remembering. Others may feel guilty because they will be late for a special dinner their spouse has been planning for weeks and they believe that guilt will teach them a lesson in punctuality. Yet some others may use the detour they're forced to take as an opportunity to do something in the neighborhood they've been putting off for months, and thus feel a sense of accomplishment. Same event, three different responses.

In summary, it's not what happens *to* us that affects how we feel, but what we believe the event *means* to us. Therefore, if we want to change the way we feel about something, we first have to change the belief or beliefs behind our emotions.

CHANGING THE WAY WE FEEL

On the surface, it may seem logical to blame the situations and events taking place in our lives for the way they make us feel. The problem with this approach, however, is that we are presuming that in order to change the way we feel we are first going to have to correct or "fix" the situation.

For instance, if our friend is late meeting us and we become angry, we might attempt to "fix" the situation by blaming him for our anger in the hopes that it will make him be on time in the future. We think that if we are angry enough, then maybe he'll change and start conforming to our belief about punctuality. We believe that if he changes, then we will no longer be angry. However, more often than not, this approach results in a strained or even an ended relationship, which is the opposite of what we wanted.

Or we may be faced with a situation that is totally outside of our control. The stock market may take a downturn, or the company we want to work for may impose a hiring freeze, or the promotion we were hoping to get may be given to someone else. Even though we can't really change these events, we might still attempt to "fix" the situation in our minds by blaming the circumstances for how we feel.

Ultimately, when we try to "fix" a situation all we are doing is **making something or someone else responsible for the way we feel.** This approach never really solves anything, at least not in the long term, because it places the onus for our happiness on someone or something outside of our control. We can't "make" our friend be on time any more than we can "make" the stock market go up, no matter how hard we try or how upset we get. Once we recognize that it is our beliefs that determine how we react to a given situation, we will then be taking responsibility for our own feelings. We cannot control what other people do or say or what happens out there in the world, but we do have control over our own beliefs.

With the knowledge that our emotions are not hostage to outside events but are fully under the control of our beliefs, we can take responsibility for how we feel, and as a result start changing our beliefs in order to give rise to emotions that consistently empower us.

*The diagram below illustrates the difference between a blame-based response and a belief-based response. A blame-based response implies that something or someone else is responsible for the way we feel, which means that in order to change our feelings we must "fix" the situation (which is usually outside of our control). A belief-based response, on the other hand, implies that we are taking responsibility for the way we feel about what's happened to us, which means that before we can change our feelings we have to change the beliefs behind them (which are **always** under our control).*

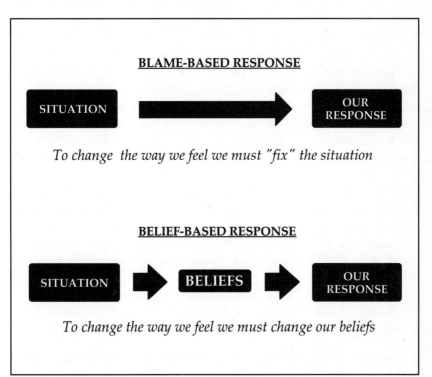

OUR BELIEFS AND OUR BEHAVIOR

Since our beliefs influence the way we feel about something, by extension they also influence our behavior towards it. For example, if we are overcharged for an item at the grocery store, our beliefs will influence how we feel about the situation which will, in turn, impact on our behavior. If we believe that we have been treated unfairly (the belief), we'll likely get angry (the feeling), and return to the store to demand our money back (the behavior). If, on the other hand, we believe that we should "never ruffle any feathers" (the belief), we'll probably feel intimidated by the prospect of going back and confronting the cashier (the feeling), and instead try to forget about the whole thing (the behavior). If we happen to have both beliefs, then the strongest one will dominate.

The power of our belief system and its influence on our behavior can be truly astounding. A few years ago, I was watching a TV news program where the anchor was reporting on the plight of a wheelchair-bound writer who in her late forties decided to move out of the big city and into a quaint little town away from it all. She wanted to be surrounded by nature because she thought it would heighten her inspiration and provide her with fresh air all the time. She had no clue about what was to happen next.

Unbeknownst to her, most people in this small town had the belief that being in a wheelchair was a punishment from God and therefore a sign of bad fortune. This belief, which had been acquired through their religious upbringing, caused them to judge her presence as an omen, a sign that evil things would soon start happening to them. As a result, very few people dared to approach her at all. When she went down the street, most people crossed to the other side so they wouldn't have to share the same sidewalk. After a while, they started pressing this poor woman to move away because they were afraid that her "bad fortune" was going to "spread" to the rest of the town.

The people of this town couldn't see a person who was just like them; they saw a punishment. Their beliefs had turned a simple wheelchair and the person riding it into something frightening to be avoided at all cost. The judgments they made about this woman were not based on facts, but on the limited beliefs they had. It is these beliefs which dramatically affected their behavior towards her.

In essence, **our behavior is a reflection of our beliefs.** Ultimately, if we want to make a lasting change in our behavior, we need to identify and then change the beliefs behind it. Mind you, this doesn't mean that we can't change our behavior *until* we change our beliefs. We can consciously change our behavior at any time (the choice is always ours). However, for this change to be *lasting* we also have to change our beliefs.

As we have learned so far, our beliefs have the powerful ability to shape what we see, how we feel about it, and the actions we choose to take as a result. Now that we know the significant influence that our beliefs have on our lives, we can only begin to imagine how eliminating those that limit us can profoundly (and permanently!) increase the quality of our lives.

THE OPPOSITE RULES!

POPULAR RULE		OPPOSITE RULE
"I have to see it to believe it."	➡	"I have to believe it in order to see it."
Everybody experiences a common reality.	➡	Each person perceives their own version of reality based on their beliefs.
The way we feel is the result of the events we witness.	➡	The way we feel about an event we witness is a consequence of our beliefs about it, and not the result of the event itself.
We can change our behavior without having to change our beliefs.	➡	Because our beliefs influence our behavior, we can't really make a *lasting* change in our behavior until we change the beliefs behind it.

EXPERIMENT:
IDENTIFYING A SELF-IMPOSED BARRIER

This experiment serves to help you clarify what beliefs you may have that might be holding you back.

* Write down something you would really like to have in your life but right now you don't (perhaps a new job, start a relationship, buy a car):

_____

* If it's something you've wanted for awhile, but "haven't gotten around to it," ask yourself why you don't have it?

_____

_____

_____

These reasons reflect limiting beliefs about what you want (perhaps you're afraid of the unknown of a new job, or enjoy your independence, or don't have enough money)

* Write down what you think the limiting belief is (you can use the list of limiting beliefs on page 22 as a reference):

_____

_____

CHAPTER 1.4
THE POWER OF PERCEPTION

In the previous chapter we learned that what we see may not necessarily be what's right in front of us, but our "perception" of it. In this chapter, we are going to take a more in-depth look at how our perception mechanism creates our individual version of reality, and we are going to learn how to use this knowledge to help us unearth limiting beliefs from our upbringing.

FICTION VS. REALITY

I am a big fan of Steven Spielberg. Of all his movies, I especially enjoyed *Jurassic Park*. What I liked so much about it was how it managed to present a premise that is unrealistic—to genetically breed dinosaurs in the lab—in a very realistic and believable way. One of my favorite scenes in the movie takes place near the beginning when the paleontologists are visiting Jurassic Park for the first time and have their first close encounter with a living dinosaur. These scientists had been working all their lives to learn more about how the mysterious dinosaurs lived, mainly based on a few fossils and a lot of guess work. But now here they were, looking at the long-extinct creatures parading in front of their incredulous faces. One of the scientists was so profoundly taken aback by the sight that he lost the strength in his legs and fell to the ground in total awe.

While I found *Jurassic Park's* story line fascinating, what I found even more fascinating was the effect this movie had on people. Inside the theater, it captured the imagination of entire audiences. But outside the theater, it captured the imagination of the world.

All of a sudden there was a renewed interest in the study of dinosaurs. Every major museum of science opened a dinosaur exhibit. Most schools beefed up their curriculums to focus on the dinosaur age at the overwhelming request of children. An NBA franchise picked the name and image of a dinosaur for their new basketball team. Companies started incorporating dinosaurs into their advertising campaigns. New books, games, toys, posters, software—anything featuring dinosaurs—flooded the marketplace. I would even venture to guess that most professors studying paleontology probably found it much easier to obtain research grants during this time!

The funny thing is that while all of these events were very real, neither the story, the characters, nor the dinosaurs in *Jurassic Park* were "real." The story was a thrilling piece of science fiction, the characters were fictitious, and the dinosaurs themselves were a combination of props and sophisticated computer software.

So, how could a piece of fiction create so much reality around it? After all, a lot of people the world over invested "real" time and "real" money in order to satisfy their new-found interest in dinosaurs. Clearly, *Jurassic Park* wasn't the first movie ever to feature these creatures; however, what this movie did do for the first time was to create an image of realism never before achieved. For a full two hours, *Jurassic Park* **was** real to the audience, not because the dinosaurs used in the movie were alive and kicking, but because the people in the audience **chose to believe** the image of realism presented to them on the screen.

This choice accounts for the reaction of the audiences. For instance, they responded with exhilaration when the dinosaurs first appeared, fear when the characters in the movie were under attack, and relief when the characters finally managed to escape the island unharmed. The nature and intensity of the audiences' feelings were as real to them as any feeling of exhilaration, fear, or relief they might experience in their personal lives.

It seems that we have the ability to <u>choose</u> what we will accept as our reality. Whether we see a group of images on a movie screen or read a story in a novel, we seem to have the ability to make any of these as real in our minds as something that we experience in our own lives. All it takes is for us to *believe* the plot in the movie or to *believe* the story in the novel. Whether the events represented actually took place or not is really inconsequential.

What determines primarily whether we accept something as real or not is our decision to believe in it, not the authenticity of the event.

What's fascinating about the above observation is the way we apply it in our daily routine. When we go about our lives, we constantly make up and play "movies" in our minds. For example, if we seem unable to earn more than a certain level of income no matter how hard we try, then we may subconsciously choose to play the "Everybody Is Out to Get Me" movie in our mind. The characters in this movie might be our boss, our spouse, our family, our friends, or all of the above. In our eyes, these characters play the tormenting role of putting us down, patronizing us, or telling us we don't have what it takes to earn more than we do. Whether these people are actually behaving in this way or not doesn't matter. These are the roles *we* have cast them in and they are playing the script *we* have written. We may not be fully aware that we are playing these movies in our minds, but like real movies, we believe them (since *we* have created them subconsciously) and as a result they become real to us.

Let's now take a look at the process by which we make these movies in our minds, so that we can learn how to use them to our benefit.

THE PERCEPTION LENS

Our "movie-making" begins with our perception mechanism. As we learned in the previous chapter, the way we see reality (our own perception) is the result of our beliefs filtering, changing, and reshaping the information coming through our senses. A good way to explain how our perception mechanism works is to make an analogy with a lens. When we look at an object through a lens, what we see is not the object itself but an image of it. This image may not necessarily be a true representation of the original, but depending on how the lens is designed, the object might look magnified, shrunk, or distorted. Even the color of the object can change if the lens is tinted. Similarly in our lives, when we observe something, we are not looking at it directly but through our "perception lens." This lens is located in our mind and it constantly alters what comes through our senses.

How do these lenses work? In the case of an optical lens, the way an object will look through it is determined by the design of the lens. The same principle applies to our "perception lens," except that in this case the designer of the lens is our belief system.

Our beliefs can tint, distort, magnify, or reduce, anything that comes through our five senses.

Now that we have a basic understanding about how our perception mechanism works, let's explain why we have the need to make "movies" in our mind.

A significant part of our daily lives consists of making sense of what we see and what we hear. This is critical for our survival. If we were unable to make sense of our world, then we would be unable to communicate with it. Without communication, our mental health would be at risk. For example, in the old days, solitary confinement chambers in U.S. jails resembled a bank safe more than a prison cell in that they had no lights, no heat, and were designed to be soundproof. As a result of the total lack of communication, inmates who were kept in them for long periods of time would become temporarily insane.

To prevent a similar situation from happening in our own lives, our survival mechanism (our belief system) automatically kicks in to preserve our sanity whenever we are unable to make sense of the events surrounding us. The way it achieves this task is by altering our sense of reality—i.e. creating a mental "movie"—so that we can quickly regain control over the world around us. As mentioned in a previous example, if we can't understand why we are unable to earn more than we presently make no matter how hard we try, then we may subconsciously create the "Everybody Is Out to Get Me" movie in our mind in order to bring sense back into our circumstances. In essence, we are using our perception mechanism to "manufacture" a reality that fulfills our sense of survival.

Now, these made-up movies may allow us to survive in the world, but they may not necessarily support our growth since they are based on the beliefs we have at the time. If our movies are based on limiting beliefs, then we'll behave in a limiting way and we'll create limiting roles for the "actors" in them (the people in our lives). **In order to create new movies where we feel that the "script" and "characters" in them support us, we must have beliefs that support us as well.** By replacing our limiting beliefs with empowering ones, we'll be establishing the basis for creating movies in our mind that support our growth.

WHEN WE PLAY SOMEBODY ELSE'S ROLES

In addition to making our own movies, oftentimes we are made to play "roles" in other people's "movies." We may not necessarily be aware that we are playing these characters, since they only exist in the minds of the movie makers (who are themselves, more often than not, unaware of them).

However, if these people are in a position of authority or are emotionally attached to us, oftentimes we are unwillingly made to play the characters they need us to become. This is usually achieved through mental games and manipulation. Many of the limiting beliefs that we developed when we grew up were the result of being in somebody else's "movie." If we were made to play some "character" in a movie made by somebody in a position of authority, we had no recourse but to comply with the "script."

Eleven-year-old Andrea had a crush on a boy at school named Drew who sat behind her. They would talk sometimes during class and joke with each other, both of them learning how to flirt with the opposite sex. The teacher got tired of telling them to be quiet so she separated them. Andrea was moved to a desk near the middle of the class while Drew was moved to the back. Sometimes, Drew would whisper her name and say something. She couldn't quite catch it the first few times, but she soon heard him clearly, "Pssst. Andrea, you're a tease." Andrea had never heard that word before, but to her, it was just another flirting term. So she smiled back in response. One day, Andrea mentioned the word to her older sister and the fact that Drew was addressing her with it. The next day her father stormed into her room screaming at her that no boy was to call her a tease and that she was to make him apologize immediately. Suddenly, the word that had been a term of endearment became the reason for war with this boy she really liked. To appease her father, Andrea, in terror, went to school and demanded he apologize to her. He refused.

For weeks, school was a very uncomfortable place for Andrea. So her friends taught her a new word to get back at Drew: prick. She began calling him "prick" because that was the only way she felt she could defend her honor. These two kids who had had an innocent attraction for each other now became caught in a war of words: "Tease!" "Prick!" "Tease!" "Prick!" What did these words mean? The kids didn't really know, but what they did know is that they were words to be avoided at all costs.

Andrea was made to play a character in her father's movie, called "Other People's Opinions Are More Important Than Anything Else." To him, the word "tease" was antithetical to the role he had cast her in: the role of "Innocent Virgin." So he made sure his daughter defended her role. It didn't matter that Andrea was being put into an uncomfortable position. It didn't matter what the context for the comment was, nor his daughter's feelings for the boy. All that mattered was wiping out that word because it implied that his daughter had a blossoming sexuality.

Her father's reaction made Andrea's situation at school be unnecessarily blown out of proportion. Other classmates got involved as well as the teacher. In addition, Drew was at the stage where he craved attention. When he saw that his behavior was getting a big reaction out of Andrea, he called her a tease more often. It's only when the titillating aspect of this word wore off that the situation cooled down. But Andrea and Drew rarely spoke to each other after that.

While I'm not suggesting Andrea's father should have done nothing at all, what's critical about this story is how he unknowingly forced his daughter to play in one of his own mental "movies," at Andrea's expense. He never took the time to find out how Andrea felt about the boy and what Drew was saying to her. He just jumped into his own movie as the "Defender of Reputation." Because he regarded other people's opinions as more important than his daughter's feelings, Andrea was manipulated into playing out the role he chose for her in his movie.

Later, in the Relationships section of the book (Part 2), we'll address how to break the cycle of playing unwanted roles in other people's movies. While a child doesn't have much of a choice, we as adults do. As a matter of fact, it is quite useful to identify the roles we played at home, since a lot of times we keep playing these roles well into our adult lives. The experiment at the end of this chapter will show us an effective way to unearth limiting beliefs that we inherited from our upbringing by recalling the "roles" that we were made to play in our "family movies."

As we get further into our *Second Invention,* we'll be able to start taking advantage of our perception mechanism to create a version of reality that constantly serves us and helps us achieve sustained growth in our lives.

THE OPPOSITE RULES!

POPULAR RULE

What determines whether we accept something as real or not is the authenticity of the event.

➡

OPPOSITE RULE

What determines whether we accept something as real or not is our decision to believe in it. The authenticity of the event is secondary.

EXPERIMENT:
YOUR FAMILY "MOVIES"

The goal of this experiment is to start identifying limiting beliefs that you were conditioned with while growing up, specifically the "roles" you played in other people's mental "movies." Any family member in a position of authority, such as parents, older brothers and sisters, or care-givers made "movies" for themselves so they could relate to the other members of the family. A good number of the limiting beliefs developed during our upbringing came from the roles we were given at home in our "family movies."

• Try to recall past family circumstances, such as fights or arguments in which you felt uncomfortable with an authority figure. Write down two or three of those circumstances that happened periodically throughout your childhood (e.g. your father would tell you to shut up every time you tried to say something at the dinner table while the adults were talking about something).

1 _____

2 _____

3 _____

• For each circumstance, give it a movie title (e.g. "Children Should Be Seen and Not Heard") and try to figure out the "role" that you were made to play (e.g. "Quiet and Submissive Child").

1 Title: _____

   Role: _____

2 Title: _____

   Role: _____

3 Title: _____

   Role: _____

- Think about the limiting beliefs that might have been created as a result of consistently playing those childhood characters (e.g. "To be accepted by people, I have to keep my thoughts and opinions to myself"), and write them below:

1 _____

2 _____

3 _____

CHAPTER 1.5

GOOD NEWS AND BAD NEWS

Now that we have a good understanding of how our perception mechanism works in our minds, I have good news and bad news. *The good news is that the bad news is only as bad as we want to make it!*

The real difference between good news and bad news is not in the news itself, but in our positive or negative perception of it. News just takes place. Whether it is "good" or "bad" is truly up to us. For instance, the news media may go to great lengths to make their news reporting sound objective, but in the end, whenever they label a piece of news as "good" or "bad" all they are actually doing is broadcasting the perception of the news editors.

Let's illustrate this point by showing how a given event has the potential for looking either good or bad, depending on how we choose to perceive it. A recent statistic from the National Highway Traffic Safety Administration claimed that 30,000 people died in the U.S. of alcohol-related traffic accidents in 1996. As soon as we see this figure, our perception lens goes to work. Almost immediately we create in our minds an image that we label as either good or bad. If our minds are focused on the pain and suffering that thousands of families must have experienced, then we'll obviously conclude that this is a "bad" piece of news. But if our minds focus on the fact that this figure indicates that the number of alcohol-related traffic fatalities has gone down by a whopping 30% from the previous ten years, then we'll conclude that this is a "good" piece of news.

Mind you, this doesn't mean that it makes us happy to know that 30,000 people died that year of alcohol-related traffic accidents. It just means that we are pleased about the encouraging proof that the decline of drunk-driving in our society is stronger than ever. Interestingly, the original statistic didn't refer to the pain and suffering of thousands of people, nor did it refer to the fact that the number of alcohol-related traffic fatalities had gone down by 30% in ten years. It simply stated that *30,000 people died in the U.S. of alcohol-related traffic accidents in 1996.*

What is very important to realize here is that our two different interpretations don't really alter the facts claimed by the original statistic, yet they significantly alter our outlook in life. Our focus on "bad" makes us feel helpless, makes us feel scared to drive or walk on the streets, makes us feel that our society is getting more dangerous, and so on. Our focus on "good," however, makes us feel that we are evolving as a society, makes us feel hopeful, makes us feel that our society is becoming more safety conscious. In essence, the "bad" interpretation creates for us an outlook of helplessness and limitation, whereas the "good" interpretation creates an outlook of hope and progress. The statistic itself (the "news"), however, remains the same.

THE OPTIMIST, THE PESSIMIST, AND THE REALIST

I find it interesting that when we choose to have a positive outlook in life, we are often told that we are looking at things through rose-colored glasses. Presumably, we are being accused of having an unrealistic view of the world. And yet the very people who make these comments don't realize that they are looking at things through colored glasses themselves. They just happen to be wearing a darker shade than ours. Ultimately, **having a positive outlook in life is as much of a choice as having a negative one.**

When pessimists tell optimists that they are not being *realistic,* they don't realize that optimists are as realistic as pessimists, no more, no less. After all, the optimist's reality is as valid to an optimist as the pessimist's is to a pessimist.

Remember, when it comes to experiencing reality everything is subjective. If many observers are looking at the same object, each one of the observers will only see their personal "image" of the object according to their own perception. For example, one day I was shopping in one of those warehouse-style superstores for some stationery and I noticed that a bird had sneaked into the building and was flying around. While I was waiting in line at the checkout counter, a woman in her forties came running out from one of the aisles screaming and sweating profusely, dropped everything she was planning to buy, and ran in a panic out the nearest door. When I got to the checkout register, I asked the clerk if she knew what the fuss was all about, and she told me that this customer had a strong phobia of birds. She could not be in the same enclosed space with a bird without feeling terrified and trapped.

This woman and myself saw the same object, a flying bird. Yet the image in my mind was that of a beautiful black crow while the image in her mind was of a threatening creature to be avoided at all cost. Same object, two completely different interpretation of events.

Ultimately, an observer can only see his or her *own* version of reality. Therefore, when somebody tells us that we are not being *realistic,* it's a good idea to remind ourselves that their interpretation of events is not based on some universal truth, but is bound instead by the limits of their own beliefs.

Nobody can claim to have the truth, since they can never "see" it directly, but only through their own perception.

OUR "EVIDENCE"

By nature, human beings are gatherers of evidence. We compile this information to see where and how we fit in the world. We are also "generalizers." Even though most of this information comes from specific incidents in our immediate environment, we love to generalize it to the entire human race.

When people tell us to "be realistic," they are actually telling us to abide by their evidence. They believe that what their evidence doesn't support, cannot be done. As a result, they attempt to discourage us because they don't want us to challenge their beliefs. They fear that if we attempt something that they claim cannot be done and we succeed at it, our success will threaten everything they believe to be true. All of their lives they have been gathering evidence in order to support their beliefs and now they must make sure that *we* also comply with *their* requirements of reality.

Naturally, if we refuse to listen to their evidence and go for what we want anyway, they will likely tell us that we are making a terrible mistake. In the end, their response simply reflects their own limiting beliefs about what is possible in the world.

The problem, however, is that oftentimes we let ourselves get easily discouraged by these "realists." The reason we do so is that instead of investing the time and effort required to generate our own evidence, many times we resort to borrowing somebody else's. For example, if the evidence shows that everyone in John's family has always worked for someone else, it's quite likely that John will have great difficulty getting the courage to start his own business—not because John doesn't have the skill, or the talent, or the ingenuity, but because the "evidence" surrounding him does not support the concept of self-employment.

If he ever entertains the thought of going into business for himself, he is bound to be pressured to "stick to what works" and "what gives you security." Many reminders of this evidence will sneak up to dissuade him, like having to pay the mortgage, having to support the children, the car breaking down, and so on. If John believes this evidence of financial dependence, then his life will simply unfold to perpetuate it.

Now the question is, if relying on external evidence doesn't always support our dreams, then *why* do we resort so often to other people's evidence as the basis for our own? The answer is that many of us have been raised with the belief that the best way to assess how we are doing in life is to use somebody else's experiences as our yardstick; in other words, to use external events as the point of reference for our growth. However, what nobody has ever told us is that we can support our dreams much more effectively by developing our own *internal* reference point, or internal "evidence."

EXTERNAL VS. INTERNAL REFERENCE POINTS

External reference points, such as somebody else's accomplishments, somebody else's choices, somebody else's level of skill, and so on, have two main drawbacks: they *change* all the time and they are *outside* of our control. For example, if we get promoted at work from section supervisor to section manager, there will always be somebody we know (an external reference point) who will get promoted from section manager to department manager. So instead of feeling truly happy with our promotion, we manage to feel somewhat disappointed because no matter how much we advance in our career, there's always someone else doing better than we are.

Internal reference points, on the other hand, are fully under our control and, as a result, they don't change unless *we* want them to. To better illustrate the difference between internal and external reference points, let's use an analogy. Let's say that we want to assess how tall we are by looking at other people walking on the street. A man we deem to be of "average height" walks by us. Since we are taller than him, we conclude that we are taller than average, which makes us feel good. But next comes a woman who is taller than we are. Now we aren't so happy about our height anymore because all of the sudden we appear to be short. We get confused. By using external reference points to assess how tall we are, we end up setting ourselves up for a losing battle because we are dealing with a moving target.

However, if we decide to stop using the people on the street to measure our height and decide instead to buy our own measuring tape (an internal reference point), then we'll be assured that an inch yesterday was as long as an inch today and it will be as long as an inch tomorrow. Now we have a way of knowing precisely not only how tall we are, but also how much we are growing. Using an internal reference point helps us assess our progress in life without needing to compare ourselves to others. Since it doesn't change over time, we can clearly see where we stand in our lives and how much we are growing personally and professionally.

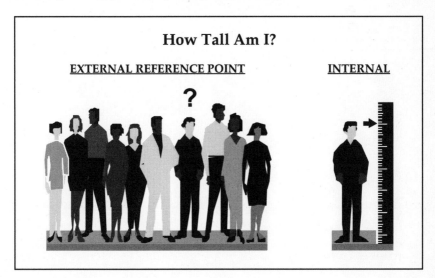

How Tall Am I?

EXTERNAL REFERENCE POINT **INTERNAL**

If, on the other hand, we use external reference points, then no matter how much we achieve in our lives we will *always* find somebody who makes more money than we do, who has a faster career path, who has a higher status, who has more knowledge in our field of expertise, who has done what we do longer than we have, and so on, and so on, and so on.

By focusing on all those external differences, we lose track of the most important thing in our quest for advancement: *ourselves*. Developing an internal reference instead will help us regain our focus on how we are doing.

How do we establish this internal reference? By starting to collect "evidence" about *our own* achievements instead of somebody else's. We need to rewrite our beliefs to focus on what makes *us* unique, what makes *us* special, what makes *us* who we are. This focus on self is necessary because it helps us to establish our own personal foundation from which we can build on.

The only way we can truly become productive and successful members of society is by taking full charge of our own personal and professional growth. But this growth won't happen as effectively if we constantly compare ourselves to others. We need to turn our attention inwards. In fact, the more we focus on our own point of reference, the more "realistic" we will be because we'll be assessing ourselves against the only evidence that matters—who we are.

THE OPPOSITE RULES!

POPULAR RULE

Whether news are good or bad depends on the nature of the news.

OPPOSITE RULE

The difference between good news and bad news isn't in the news itself, but in our positive or negative perception of it.

Using other people's experience as our yardstick is a good way to assess our growth.

Using our own experience as a yardstick is an even better way!

EXPERIMENT:
COLLECTING YOUR OWN EVIDENCE

The goal of this experiment is to start collecting "evidence" about our own development and achievements. We need to stop using somebody else's achievements to see where we are at. The "external" reference points do not serve us, except as an excuse to get discouraged if we do not meet or surpass them. To be able to truly measure our personal and professional growth, we need to develop our own "internal" reference point. Here is a good beginning:

- List all the achievements you can remember in the last ten years (e.g. a degree you obtained, a job you landed, a weight loss target you reached even if you regained some or all of it later):

_____   _____

_____   _____

_____   _____

_____   _____

_____   _____

_____   _____

_____   _____

- In the chart on the following page, divide them into the following general categories: *Personal, Professional, Health,* and *Relationships* (you can add more categories to this list, but try not to go over five, otherwise the achievements will become too scattered to have the desired effect).

- Every time you have an achievement in the course of your daily routine (no matter how small you think it is) enter it into the appropriate category. As a rule of thumb, an achievement is anything you planned to do and completed, even if took longer than anticipated.

PERSONAL

_____
_____
_____
_____
_____

PROFESSIONAL

_____
_____
_____
_____

HEALTH

_____
_____
_____
_____

RELATIONSHIPS

_____
_____
_____
_____

- Whenever you feel discouraged with something you're trying to accomplish in your life, read the above list as proof that you "have what it takes" within you to achieve whatever you set out to do. Have fun!

CHAPTER 1.6

ON THE ROAD TO ACHIEVEMENT

We are now becoming more and more aware of the central role that our belief system plays in our lives. We have learned how our beliefs are instrumental in influencing our emotions and our behavior, defining our reality through our perception, attracting our circumstances, and shaping our experience.

So far, most of us have lived our lives on auto pilot since our mostly inherited beliefs have been doing the steering for us. But with this new understanding of the different ways that our beliefs can influence our lives, we now have the necessary knowledge to finally turn the auto pilot switch off and become active pilots in our own lives.

However, knowledge alone does not make things happen. We need to be able to **apply** this knowledge in order to get the results we want. And here is where most of us tend to get stuck. We are always ready and willing to acquire new knowledge so that we can make a change in our lives. But when it comes to applying it to get the results we want, we somehow allow our readiness and willingness to get easily eroded.

In this chapter we are going to look at two of the main roadblocks that take away our motivation to get results, and we are also going to learn how to overcome them effectively.

TWO COMMON ROADBLOCKS TO ACHIEVEMENT

There are two common roadblocks that we are likely to encounter when trying to get results in our lives: the need to achieve perfection, and the tendency to look for the "holes" in what we do. These roadblocks are very effective at discouraging us from achieving our goals and, for the most part, they manage to do their "stalling" undetected. In the next few pages, we will uncover why we face these roadblocks, and what we can do to remove them permanently from our lives.

ROADBLOCK 1: THE NEED FOR PERFECTION

In our society, attaining perfection is so deeply ingrained in us, that whenever we set out to achieve something we end up imposing an incredible amount of pressure on ourselves. We feel that unless we can guarantee that we can achieve what we want with total and utter perfection, it's not worth putting a lot of effort into it.

However, most times we can't make this guarantee because we don't think we have the level of skill or the amount of time required to achieve such a high degree of perfection. So, we either do it halfheartedly and eventually give up, or we don't even attempt it in the first place. This is one of the most common and effective "dream killers" around. By trying to be perfect, we focus less and less on what we want and more and more on achieving a "perfect result." In other words, we get so obsessed about the level of perfection of our end result that we stop enjoying what we are doing altogether.

In order to start turning the "perfection" tide around, we need to counter it with beliefs that help us achieve the results we are striving for without placing the focus on "getting it perfect." An empowering belief I've come across that works wonders is the following:

You don't have to be perfect to achieve perfection.

For example, my wife recently decided to produce and star in a play she loved. Although she had done a lot of acting, she had never produced before. A die-hard perfectionist, she had her moments wondering, "What if it's not good enough?," "I've never produced before—do I really have what it takes?," "What if I make mistakes?" These questions scared her at times, but instead of letting herself get discouraged by the perfection "bug," she decided to embrace the above empowering belief as the motto for her production. She did make some mistakes, but in the end she was thrilled with the result. Audiences who saw the show raved about the performances and the overall quality of the production.

While she would be the first to admit everything wasn't perfect, she's also quick to say that she feels she achieved a level of "perfection" she had never before achieved. In the end, she did the very best she could under the circumstances and she came away from the experience having learned a lot about what she could do differently next time. But the main thing is that she pursued her want with conviction without letting the need for perfection come in the way of her enjoyment. As a result, she created a wonderful experience for herself, her staff and the audiences who saw the play.

If, instead of focusing on the perfection of the results, we focus on trying to be the best we can under our present circumstances, then most times we *will* achieve "perfect" results. Not because our results will be the best ever in the entire world, but because they'll be the best **we** have ever achieved. In hindsight, there is no universal standard for "perfection." Perfection means different things to different people (in a way, it is as subjective as our view of reality). All we have to do is to change our own definition so that perfection reflects what we can do, not the ultimate that has ever been achieved.

Most times, we do our best work when we are *not* trying to be perfect. By removing this pressure we better allow our knowledge to become second nature. When we are trying to be perfect we are too much "in our heads." We *think* too much and as a result we are unable to *do* as much. If you learned to play golf or tennis as an adult, can you remember when you were taking those first few lessons? There were so many variables involved in the perfect golf swing or the perfect tennis backhand that it was overwhelming just to think about all of them at the same time. So we took it one step at a time. We would practice one or two moves until they became second nature, and only then would we move on to the next. By the time we were done with all the variables, we didn't have to think anymore; we would just do the swing or the backhand naturally.

The same applies to our own lives. If we focus on *doing the best ever achieved,* then we'll want to conquer all the variables involved at the same time to get ultimate perfection. If my wife had focused on conquering all the variables she had to deal with at the same time in order to get "perfect results," she never would have produced the play in the first place. She would have given up way before starting because she would have felt the overwhelming pressure to "be perfect."

If, instead, we focus on *doing the best we can,* then we'll be able to do away with our need for perfection. As a result, the quality and excellence of our work will more likely achieve levels of perfection that we have never attained before.

ROADBLOCK 2: LOOKING FOR THE HOLES

The second roadblock on our road to achievement, is our tendency to "look for the holes" in our accomplishments. What I mean by this expression is that instead of placing our focus on what we have already achieved, we tend to focus on what's missing, on what's not quite there yet, on what doesn't work one hundred percent.

The problem with this way of looking at things is that no matter what we do, we'll never be truly satisfied. We are forever unhappy because we know we could always have done it better.

Looking for the holes is a side-effect of our quest for ultimate perfection. We think that if we only focus on what has already been done, then we'll forget about what is still missing and therefore never "make it right." But we know now that this is just a belief. A limiting belief. We can accomplish much more if we are happy for what we have done instead of being unhappy for what remains to be done.

Hard to believe? Let's learn from the masters of achievement themselves: young children. Just think of the number of accomplishments a young child goes through in a typical month. For instance, they learn to stand up on their own and walk for the first time after dozens and dozens of failed attempts. Can you imagine if they criticized themselves every time they stood up and fell right back on their behinds? Can you imagine if they just gave up trying to walk out of frustration and being afraid to fail again? We would all live in a society of crawlers!

Young children are naturally happy with their achievements. They never go the refrigerator door and start criticizing the drawings they have proudly made. You'll never hear them say "I wish I'd drawn arms of even length on this stick figure" or "I wish I didn't draw this girl with Picasso eyes." They are perfectly happy with the level of skill they already have. So, why can't we do this when we grow up?

Young children are able to achieve so much because they do everything from a foundation of happiness. Instead of looking for the holes in what they do, they naturally look for the fun.

We can do this too. Remember, we were all children once. We still have somewhere within us the ability to achieve for the sake of achieving, and not for the sake of not failing. We just have to reclaim this ability in our adult lives **by deciding to stop looking for the holes in what we do.** In this way we'll begin traveling again on our road to achievement the fun way we once knew, but forgot about while growing up.

Now that we have reached the end of Part 1, we have a good understanding about the power and influence that our beliefs have on our everyday lives. We now know, for instance, that our beliefs ultimately determine how we feel about ourselves and the world around us, and how we behave as a result. In the next three parts of the book, we will apply this knowledge to significantly improve the quality and enjoyment of our relationships (Part 2), our careers (Part 3), and finally our life experience as a whole (Part 4).

THE OPPOSITE RULES!

POPULAR RULE		**OPPOSITE RULE**

We have to be perfect to achieve perfection.

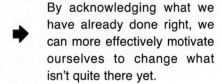

We <u>don't</u> have to be perfect to achieve perfection. We can achieve it by simply doing the best we can under the circumstances.

We have to look at what we have done wrong in order to motivate ourselves to get it right.

By acknowledging what we have already done right, we can more effectively motivate ourselves to change what isn't quite there yet.

PART ONE REVIEW

In Part 1, we have gained a clear understanding about the working of the mind and the power of our beliefs. If you have uncovered a limiting belief or two from reading the preceding chapters or from doing the preceding experiments, then write them down below (we will be using this information later on in the book):

_____

_____

_____

_____

PART 2

REINVENTING YOUR RELATIONSHIPS

*"We learn about ourselves
through our relationships"*

CHAPTER 2.1
THE MANIPULATIONSHIP

However we choose to live and wherever we choose to go, as long as we live in society, we are bound to have relationships in our lives. While our primary relationships are with our partners and families, we also have them with coworkers, relatives, neighbors, friends, business associates, our boss, the grocer, our doctor, and anyone we meet.

Given that our relationships play such an integral role in our lives, it's surprising that we were never formally taught how to relate to one another. All those years of schooling prepared us so that one day we could become productive members of society; however, they didn't necessarily teach us how to relate to the very people we would be working with, living with, and socializing with.

Since we never received any formal training on relationships, whenever we get into one, our first instinct is to repeat the patterns we acquired at home. Any patterns that we picked up during our upbringing will likely manifest in our own relationships, whether we are aware of them or not. Incidentally, these patterns didn't necessarily begin with our parents. While they were growing up, they picked them up from our grandparents, and our grandparents from our great grandparents. In hindsight, many of our relationship patterns have been in our families for generations.

Most of these patterns have changed with the times along with our evolution as a society. For instance, many harsh forms of discipline from the past have become much milder over time. But there is one relationship pattern that seems to have escaped the passage of time unscathed. This is the habit of manipulation. Manipulating others involves using their emotional attachment to us so that we can steer them in the direction we want them to go, without their consent or awareness (as a matter of fact, this technique has been so frequently used in relationships throughout history that a more fitting term for them would be *manipulationship*). The stronger the emotional attachment that two people have, the stronger the role that manipulation is likely to play in their relationship. Typically, the highest level of emotional attachment is found in married couples, followed closely by our immediate families. After all, it's the people who are closest to us who know best how to push our buttons.

Keep in mind that emotional attachment does not necessarily imply being "emotional." For instance, some couples manipulate each other using coldness and distance. Hardly any emotion is expressed because they know on a subconscious level that lack of emotion gets the results they are after. However, they are still using the emotional connection they have to manipulate each other.

In most cases, we don't even realize when we are manipulating our partner. This happens because we are not typically aware of the inherited beliefs that are making us behave in this way. Becoming aware of why and how we use manipulation to get what we want is the first step towards reinventing our relationships.

UNDERSTANDING MANIPULATION

Mind games, power plays, and guilt are all different forms of manipulation used for achieving the same result: *Getting what we want at somebody else's expense*. While there is nothing wrong with going for and getting what we want, what's wrong is doing it at somebody's **expense** because we are taking away their freedom to do what *they* want to do. Naturally, both partners in a relationship are partly responsible for manipulation to work because it cannot exist unless both people play the game. That said, using manipulation is not conducive to a supporting and nurturing relationship because neither person is being truly honest about their wants. Ultimately, all we end up doing is perpetuating a constant state of mistrust. Over time this mistrust gradually erodes our relationships, and if taken too far it can even cause serious and irreversible damage.

> *Manipulation is a way of using our emotional attachment with people to coerce them into giving us what we want.*

A friend of mine once told me a fascinating story about the long-term effects of manipulation. In his early days as an alternative medicine practitioner, he was asked to treat a woman in her fifties who had a severe case of arthritis that had started in her arms and then spread to almost her entire body. My friend was called in as a last resort, since none of the conventional medical treatments she had been through seemed to improve her condition. He treated her for a while, but in spite of his best efforts, he couldn't help to lessen her pain. She would become better temporarily and then, soon after, relapse to her advancing condition. Eventually, they discontinued the treatments since they didn't seem to be effective.

A few years later, my friend bumped into the woman's husband, now a widower, who related to him the story of their lives together. When they had met, he had been a career military officer, while she had been a concert violinist. After several years of marriage, they realized that for him to have a successful career, he would have to be highly mobile, which meant he would have to be stationed in many different bases a few years at a time. His wife, however, had a promising career as a concert violinist and didn't want to give it up. Her career required her to stay in the city where they lived at the time because she had already established a professional reputation and a network of valuable contacts in her field.

Nevertheless, he somehow managed to convince her to give up her career and follow him wherever his military career took them. He shared the then common belief in the military that the wives of career officers were "expected" to follow their husbands. As a result, she felt pressured to follow him, even though this was against her better judgment.

Apparently, they had a normal life together for many years while he was doing active duty—until he retired, that is. Eventually, they moved back to the city they had lived in those first few years of marriage. At this point, he was in his sixties while she was in her fifties. Almost as soon as they settled back, she started developing what quickly became a severe case of arthritis. The pain and suffering started in her arms and rapidly spread to almost her entire body. No matter how many doctors they saw and no matter how many different forms of therapy she was exposed to, nothing seemed to work to alleviate her worsening condition. Eventually, she died of her illness.

Afterwards, this man spent a lot of time thinking. He thought about their life together, the painful last few years, and about her illness. Finally, one day it dawned on him why their life together had ended so prematurely and so tragically.

He realized that since he had convinced her to leave her career as a concert violinist, she must have spent all those years bottling up deep feelings of resentment towards him. While he could never know for certain the truth about these feelings, he figured that there were two strong reasons for her feeling resentful: first, because he made her "agree" to give up her promising dream; and second, because she was witnessing the success of his own career, a success that she was denied. Perhaps she didn't want her feelings of resentment to interfere with his military career and that was why she never brought them out into the open. Perhaps she felt partly responsible for having agreed to follow him around.

This man felt he now understood why his wife's illness developed so rapidly soon after he retired from active duty. Something inside of her decided that there was no need for her to hide her resentment any longer, and that it was time to feel the pain of losing her dream out in the open. As a result, he believed, her condition of severe arthritis sprang up quickly and without warning. Sadly, it affected her first in both her arms, which would have been the tools of her success as a concert violinist had she been allowed to pursue her dream.

Although this is a story with a tragic ending, this example illustrates the effect that manipulation can have on somebody's life. Unfortunately, this story is not that uncommon. Many times, illnesses or medical conditions like this one are attributed to genetics, old age, or unknown causes. Perhaps a lot of them result from these factors, but in looking at how powerful our mind is, we can only ask ourselves, how many of these cases are purely physical and how many have their roots in unresolved issues within our minds? This is impossible to guess because very few people are willing to look at their lives honestly and see the beliefs that might have started an illness in the first place.

This man, courageous though he was to look at his role in his wife's experience, realized it too late to help her, but his story could be a lesson for us all. The suffering and pain that he and his wife endured might have been prevented, if only they had known that there are more effective means of pursuing our wants in a relationship than manipulation.

WHY WE MANIPULATE

Manipulation started back when we were very young. As children, we were often given a reward in exchange for doing something we *didn't* want to do. If our parents wanted us to make our beds, and we refused, they might have offered us a special dessert as our prize. This, in essence, was an early form of manipulation: "You do this for me and I'll give you something you really want." While it proved to be an easy way for our parents to get us to do something, it taught us the basics of how to pull someone's strings in order to get what we wanted.

Since as children we didn't have the ability or the resources to offer rewards in order to get what we wanted out of our parents, we learned to manipulate them by taking advantage of their weaknesses. For instance, we knew that crying got attention. What's more, the harder we cried, the more concerned our parents would become and the more they would do anything to make us feel better. Thus, crying became a powerful way to get what we wanted. Interestingly, as soon as we got it, our tears would "mysteriously" disappear.

Michael was promised that if he went to run some errands with his mother, he would get whatever he wanted from the vending machine. While they waited in line he said he wanted chocolate-covered peanuts, but when he got to the machine he saw that the other boy ahead of him had gotten the last package. Michael started crying profusely screaming that he wanted the peanuts. His mother tried to entice him with other candy, but the other kinds wouldn't do. He *only* wanted chocolate-covered peanuts! So his mother asked the other boy if he wouldn't mind exchanging his candy for hers. The other boy agreed and as soon as Michael had the chocolate-covered peanuts in his hot little hands, the tears dried up and the crying stopped. That's classic manipulation in action.

As a result of these childhood experiences, we grew up with the belief that manipulating others is a very effective way of getting what we want. Since, as adults, we have the autonomy and resources to do what we want on our own, we resent it when someone else appears to be stopping us from getting it. For example, we know that if we are alone and we want to see a particular movie, all we have to do is go to the movie theater and buy a ticket. However, if we happen to be in a relationship and our partner doesn't want to see the movie that *we* want to see, we might get upset because we are not getting what we want. Being upset is a programmed response from our early childhood. In essence, our partners have become our restrictive parents from so many years ago. In response to their "unfair" restrictions, we simply do what we were trained to do: we manipulate them into doing what we want, against their consent. While we may not use tears because we don't want to appear childish, we may use more sophisticated and "adult" tactics such as guilt, emotional distance, or ultimatums. Often, these tactics work because our partners have been programmed to respond to manipulation just as much as we have been programmed to use it.

Manipulation may get us what we want in the short term, but eventually those being manipulated will tire of always giving in and will start to resent us. If the pattern continues, our relationships will begin to get eroded, and in extreme cases we may even end up paying the consequences with our health or the health of someone we love.

So, how do we kick the habit of manipulation from our lives? How can we go for what we want without doing it at somebody else's expense? The answer to these questions lies in learning how to pursue our wants without *needing* them to be fulfilled. It is when we *need* something that our emotions kick in and we start manipulating others. In essence, we've got to learn how to **go for what we want without attaching our emotions to getting it.**

At first, it may be difficult to accept this concept because we can't imagine ourselves *not* being emotionally attached to the outcome we desire. We believe that if we don't have strong enough feelings about getting what we want, then we probably don't really want it in the first place. The problem is that more often than not, we tend to confuse "want" with "need." When we are emotionally attached to a certain outcome, our attachment doesn't actually come out of *wanting* it; it comes out of *needing* it. This need stems from a void that exists deep inside of us where we feel that if we don't get what we are looking for, our sense of self will be threatened. We feel that we *have* to get something so badly that, if we don't, we'll be devastated.

A friend of mine was preparing to audition for the three top theater schools in North America. She spent months working with her coach on her acting technique. When the time came to audition, she felt incredibly nervous because it seemed that everything was riding on this for her. She had spent all her time preparing for those key auditions and she felt she had nothing else if they didn't pan out.

She finally auditioned and a month later received three letters of rejection. None of the schools wanted her! She was devastated. She had poured her heart and soul into these auditions and it seemed as if her dreams of becoming an actor were going out the window. After two months of depression, she woke up one morning and realized that she never really *wanted* to attend the schools; she *needed* to be accepted by them. She didn't really want to go to school to become a better actor, but to get a stamp of approval that she was indeed good enough to "make the cut." In other words, she had attached her self-esteem to whether or not the schools accepted her. And this need became her recipe for failure because not getting in seriously threatened her sense of self.

Whenever we personalize our wants and make feeling good about ourselves contingent on achieving them, our wants become needs. Consequently, if we don't get what we want we become very unhappy. But this unhappiness is of our own making. My friend didn't really "have" to go to those schools—her insecurities made her *think* she did, which may be a clue for us the next time we feel anxious about achieving a want. Maybe we don't *want* it after all, but we feel we *need* it in order to fulfill some insecurity.

Anxious feelings about achieving something can be clues that a want we have is actually a need.

In our relationships, we tend to use our needs to try to manipulate others into giving us something because we have attached feeling good about ourselves to filling a void in us. Since we are convinced that we need this, we make ourselves (and others) very unhappy if we don't get it. Once we learn how to separate our needs from our wants, we'll be less inclined to use manipulation as a tool for getting what we want since our emotions will no longer be attached to the outcome.

WHEN WE ARE MANIPULATED

Many of us have felt manipulated at one time or another, but we often don't realize it until it's too late. Somebody may persuade us to do something that we don't really want to do, only to realize once we are doing it that we've been manipulated. It can be anything from our partners "making us" mow the lawn when we would rather be reading the paper, to our children "convincing" us to do their homework when they suspiciously aren't feeling well.

While there's nothing wrong with the people in our lives wanting things from us, it's an entirely different thing when they are trying to manipulate us in order to get them. More often than not, they are not even aware they are doing it because they are so accustomed to getting things this way. But we know when we are being manipulated. The most significant signs are that we feel uncomfortable with the other person's request, we have a strong desire not to do what they want, and we feel resentful. These signs are our wake-up call that we are being manipulated.

But we do have a choice. We can either do whatever it is they want us to do even though we have strong reasons why we don't want to do it, or we can stop the manipulation game in its tracks by refusing to be manipulated. It's important to note that an outright accusation of the other person as a manipulator will not help the situation because they will more often than not insist that they are not manipulating us, but simply trying to get us to do something that needs to be done. Their explanation might very well sound convincing, however our strong feelings that we are being coerced is a significant indication that we are being manipulated.

At this point, it is important for us to express that we will not do what they want us to do. Perhaps they will be angry at us, but the only way to stop feeling manipulated is for us to break the cycle. In the end, nobody can "make" us do anything. Manipulation only exists when both sides play the game. By refusing to play, we'll be taking the first step toward eradicating this harmful habit from our relationships.

BREAKING THE CYCLE

We've just learned how to stop manipulation when it is directed at us. Now the question is: How do *we* stop ourselves from manipulating others? To answer this question, we have to refer back to the difference between a *need* and a *want*. As shown in the example of my actor friend, when we need something, we are striving to fill a void inside of us. We feel a sense of emptiness that has to be filled before we can feel OK. When we manipulate others, we think we "need" to have something before we can feel good about ourselves. We think we *need* to see this particular movie tonight, we think we *need* to find the misplaced newspaper right this minute, we think we *need* our spouse to give us a ride downtown. As a result, we hold them and ourselves hostage to our own internal conflict.

In fact, we don't really *need* any of these things. We simply *want* all of these things. When we want something, we just wish to add to what we've already got. Consequently, we don't feel incomplete if we don't get it right away. We can still want something and go after it but we don't have to trick or manipulate someone else in order to get it. *We don't have to attach our emotions to getting it.* In this way, if we don't get exactly what we want, we won't be upset or unhappy.

In essence, by changing the way we perceive our desires through turning our needs into *wants*, we can begin to let go of the urge to manipulate.

A want reflects our desire to add to what we've already got, whereas a need reflects a desire to fill a void in us.

Some time ago I wanted to see a movie that had just come out called *Trial and Error,* but my wife didn't want to see it. While I was momentarily disappointed because she didn't want what *I* wanted, I decided that I didn't "need" to see this particular movie on this particular night, and that it was more important to see something else that we'd both enjoy.

Since I decided that not getting what I wanted wouldn't create a void in my life, I didn't try to manipulate my wife into doing something she didn't want to—for instance by making her feel guilty for my disappointment. Because I didn't have an emotional attachment to seeing this movie, I ended up truly enjoying the other one instead. A short time later, *Trial and Error* opened in a second run theater close to where we live, and I went to see it by myself one evening when my wife was working late.

In the end, I got to see the movie I originally wanted to, I didn't manipulate my wife, I didn't feel angry or unhappy, my wife didn't feel resentful, and I got to really enjoy another movie that I would have eventually seen anyway! Everything we both wanted was achieved at no emotional cost to myself, my wife, or our relationship.

It is really this simple. However, what may not be that simple is to replace our long lived habit of "needing" with one of "wanting." The experiment at the end of this chapter will help us start making this change in our everyday lives, so that we stop using manipulation as a way of getting what we want. The switch may not happen overnight. But be patient. As we progress, we will begin to notice that we are using manipulation less and less in our relationships and also that we are feeling manipulated less and less.

THE OPPOSITE RULES!

POPULAR RULE	**OPPOSITE RULE**
We can't get what we want unless we attach our emotions to getting it.	We CAN get what we want without attaching our emotions to getting it.

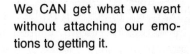

EXPERIMENT:
CHANGING NEEDS INTO WANTS

The goal of this experiment is to start undoing our habit of
"needing" things and replace it with one of "wanting" things instead
(as a rule of thumb, a need is something that evokes feelings of
anxiety and stress, whereas a want is something that evokes feelings
of excitement and fun). This replacement is necessary for us to learn
not to attach our emotions to getting what we want. Once we develop
our new habit of "wanting" things in our lives, we'll discover that
we can still get what we want in our relationships, but without the
high emotional cost of manipulation.

- List four things you feel you need (e.g. the cap on the toothpaste
  must always be on—otherwise you get upset):

  1 _____

  2 _____

  3 _____

  4 _____

- For each item, list the main reason why you feel you need it (e.g.
  your mother would get upset every time you left the cap off):

  1 _____

  2 _____

  3 _____

  4 _____

- This week, whenever these "needs" aren't fulfilled, **be aware** of
  your feelings (anger, frustration) and the underlying reasons you
  have for needing them. See if this changes how you feel about
  them.

- Experiment with making these needs your wants instead.
  Experience not being emotionally attached to achieving these
  wants and see how it feels.

CHAPTER 2.2
IS MEANING WELL GOOD ENOUGH?

Steve is in grade 12. Last year, his marks were fairly average, mostly Cs, some Ds and a few Bs. But this year they have taken a turn for the worse. He is failing a lot of tests and feels unmotivated at school. He doesn't want to talk about his situation and when his parents ask him if there is anything wrong, he tells them that he's fine and asks them to leave him alone.

Steve's parents care for him and want to help him do better in school. His dad is a problem-solver by nature. He tries to help him the best way he knows how, by suggesting ways to improve his marks, by trying to get him interested in school again and by volunteering to help him with his school work. His mom is the motivator in the family. She tells him that if he really applies himself he will have a bright future, and reminds him that since he was able to have good marks last year, he can certainly do it again this year.

Steve's parents truly mean well. They are trying to help him in any way they can. But none of the suggestions or encouragement seem to make him feel any more motivated. On the contrary, they make him feel criticized, upset and even more unmotivated.

Mike and Cindy have been married four and a half years. Lately they have been hitting some rough spots, so Mike wants to do something to improve things between them. He decides to book a romantic getaway weekend and surprise her when she comes home from work.

When Cindy gets home, he tells her about the wonderful weekend he has planned for them, but instead of reacting with delight she reacts with shock and gets very angry at him. Mike is totally confused and feels that his spirit of generosity has been completely betrayed.

When it comes to relating to our loved ones, we always mean well. We try to give them our love in whatever way we are able to. We try to do what we think is best for them and give them our best advice. Naturally, we expect some kind of appreciation and gratitude in return for our efforts. But oftentimes, we get quite the opposite reaction and we don't understand why. After all, if we mean well, at least our efforts should be acknowledged. We may not be perfect in our approach, but at least we are trying to do something good. How, then, can our positive intentions ever be interpreted as negative?

To answer this question we first need to look at the way we usually carry out our positive intentions in our relationships. When we are trying to help or do something for others, we tend to assume that we fully understand how they are feeling and that we know what they can do to fix their problems. We believe that what works for us must also work for them. Unfortunately, it doesn't always work that way. When we claim that we have the solution to other people's problems, we are presupposing that our beliefs are the same as theirs. In other words, we assume that our beliefs are universal, and since they have helped us with our lives, they will automatically help other people with theirs.

But everybody has their own set of beliefs, which makes them —and by extension their problems—unique. So it is not that unusual that a belief we hold as right for ourselves may be wrong for someone else. Actually, this situation is more common than not. *The key to successful relationships is to be able to accept this fact of life and to learn to use it for the benefit of all involved.*

Different beliefs call for different solutions.

Even if we stick to our guns and try to force or manipulate a resolution, the issue we think is "taken care of" will likely come up again and again until it is truly resolved. For instance, Steve's parents may finally get him to study and improve his marks, and think that everything is fine, until the next time he has trouble. If they don't let Steve find his own answer, but instead force their answer on him, the problem will likely recur.

To truly make a change in our relationships, we have to be able to let go of the old habit of solving someone else's problems and instead help them find their own solutions. In this way, we'll be taking our relationships to higher levels of understanding, cooperation, and communication.

RESOLVING CONFLICTS IN OUR RELATIONSHIPS

There are many books on the subject of relationships and many more tried and tested techniques on conflict resolution. However, if we analyze most of these techniques, we'll find that they follow a few common patterns. Basically, they can be summarized into three key realities of relationships. These realities, added to our good intentions, can go a long way towards eliminating most of the friction and misunderstandings in our relationships:

FIRST REALITY:
IT'S THE ACTION, NOT US, THAT ISN'T GOOD ENOUGH

When we do something with good intentions, we may find it very hard to accept that what we have done or said isn't "good enough." After all, when we mean well, it's very natural to feel hurt and confused if the other person doesn't receive our efforts as we wish they would. The reason we feel this way is that we are taking the rejection personally. Mike may think: "How could Cindy be so ungrateful after all the time and expense I took to put this trip together! I can't believe she's taking me for granted in this way." He is assuming that she feels *he* is not good enough, when more likely it's his action that isn't good enough *right now*. If he indulges in his feelings of rejection, then he'll make it very difficult for both of them to get to the core of Cindy's issue, since all of his focus will be on himself and his hurt feelings.

If a well-meant gesture backfires on us, we have to accept that it's the action we took that isn't good enough, not that *we* aren't good enough. What's important about this distinction is that if we feel that we aren't good enough ourselves, then we are not going to be in a good frame of mind to get to the real root of the problem. However, if we can just accept that what we did is not working *and* understand that what happened to us does not constitute a personal rejection, then we can release our hurt and be free to focus on the real issue.

For instance, Steve's parents have to be able to accept the fact that their efforts, however well intended, are not helping their son. Mike has to be able to accept the fact that a getaway weekend is not going to make the rough spots in his relationship disappear. The reasons why these efforts are not working are still unknown to them (we'll show you how to uncover them in the next two realities of relationships), but if they understand that it's their actions and not themselves that are being rejected, then they will be in a much better position to find out what the *real* problem is.

Accepting that our actions may not be good enough and NOT that we aren't good enough is the first step towards resolving a conflict.

SECOND REALITY:
EVERYBODY HAS DIFFERENT BELIEFS

No matter who we are and who we are with, we all have different beliefs. Our beliefs are what makes us unique. Can you imagine if everybody had exactly the same beliefs? We would all probably be a carbon copy of each other. There would be no variety, no originality, no individualism. Acknowledging this reality can do wonders for our relationships. When we appreciate people for their uniqueness instead of their conformity, we are giving them the freedom to be themselves. And this freedom is at the core of the most fulfilling relationships.

So, why do we sometimes find it so difficult to be ourselves and to let others be? The main reason is that we are afraid that unless we "belong" we will be isolated. Consequently, we either try to be somebody we are not in order to fit in or, if we are in a position of power, we force our beliefs on the people around us to make them fit to our mold. In order to dispel this fear, we have to learn to accept the fact that by nature everybody has different beliefs and will, therefore, act and respond differently than we do. Once we are able to appreciate this fact of life, we'll realize that the uniqueness of the people in our relationships are there to be celebrated, not to be used as a source of antagonism.

At first, it may be difficult for Steve's parents to accept that their son has different beliefs than they do—after all, they've raised him. But it's only when they accept him for who he is and where he is at (even if he is not meeting his potential), that they can begin to help him effectively.

Accepting that others have different beliefs than we do is the second step towards resolving a conflict.

If we develop this new habit in our lives, then any relationship that might have been a burden in the past will become energizing instead. And the best thing is that we don't need to expend a lot of effort making this happen. All we really have to do is to *decide to accept people for who they are instead of rejecting them for who they are not.*

THIRD REALITY:
PEOPLE WANT TO BE UNDERSTOOD

We can help people much more effectively by trying to understand them, than by trying to solve their problems. Since other people have different beliefs than we do, they'll have a significantly better chance of solving their problems if they look for their own answers.

When we act as problem-solvers, all we are doing is suggesting a solution based on *our* perspective of *their* problems, which means trying to solve them based on our beliefs and not theirs. Two things are ineffective about this approach. First, if we want our solutions to work for them, we have to be able to see *their* problems from *their* perspective (which won't happen if we come up with the solutions before we have put ourselves in their shoes). Second, if we are the ones coming up with the solutions all the time, then we are conditioning our loved ones to depend on us for solving their problems instead of helping them to become their own problem-solvers. A much more effective way of helping them is to act as a facilitator that coaches them to come up with their own solutions.

The secret to looking at things from somebody else's perspective is to start listening. When we are trying to help someone with a problem, we have to turn off our judgment-making machine and simply "be there" for them. People want to be listened to, not judged or told what to do or not to do, even if that's what we think they are asking for. And more often than not, they'll be very appreciative that we care enough to take the time to listen, which will ultimately make our relationships stronger.

Listening to others and trying to understand them brings us closer to a resolution.

Let's see how these three key realities of relationships can work together to help Mike and Cindy resolve their issue.

There could have been a hundred different reasons why Cindy reacted so strongly to Mike's surprise getaway trip, and yet none of those reasons might have been resolved by getting away. Maybe she felt that he always tries to fix their problems with sex and romance instead of trying to talk things through, or maybe she felt angry that he forgot her sister was coming to visit that weekend and she was reminded of the fact that he never really listens to her. If Mike takes Cindy's rejection personally and gets angry because she is not appreciating his efforts, he will lose out on an opportunity to really discover why she is upset.

Conversely, if Mike puts into practice the above three realities of relationships, he will be in a much better position to help solve their relationship issue. For instance, he will realize that:

#1• It is his action, not him, that isn't good enough.
After accepting that his action, no matter how well intended, didn't help Cindy, he can acknowledge his feelings of hurt and confusion and realize that it's not him personally who isn't good enough. Once he can accept that his getaway trip may not be the answer to their relationship problems, he can then:

#2• Accept that Cindy has different beliefs than he does.
After he realizes and accepts that she thinks and acts differently than he does, and that there is nothing wrong with that, he can begin to:

#3• Try to understand Cindy's perspective.
By listening to her, he will be helping her find the reason or reasons behind her outburst, and she will appreciate that he's making an effort to understand her.

Through using these methods, Mike will most likely discover the real reason why Cindy reacted so negatively to his surprise trip. As a result, they can begin to work out whatever issue was behind her reaction, and then maybe even end up going on the weekend he had originally planned to celebrate their revitalized relationship!

Relationships can sometimes be very confusing. We do something for someone else thinking it's good for them and it turns out to be the wrong thing. The solution, however, isn't to stop doing things for our loved ones out of a fear that they might get upset, but to be open to explore why our attempts aren't sometimes well received. It is in making an effort to understand the people we love that our relationships grow stronger.

THE OPPOSITE RULES!

POPULAR RULE

As long as we mean well, people should appreciate our efforts.

➡

OPPOSITE RULE

Meaning well is only the beginning. We also have to accept that other people have different beliefs than we do and that they want to be understood.

EXPERIMENT BREAK!

CHAPTER 2.3

COMMUNICATING VS. TALKING

The main cause of misunderstandings in relationships is poor communication. Most of us have the potential for communicating effectively, but we tend to do it poorly because we aren't really clear about what communication really entails. In this chapter, we'll learn how to begin tapping into this potential so that we can effectively stop misunderstandings before they even start to develop.

Most people think that "talking" and "communicating" are the same thing. But there are many relationships where the partners talk all the time and yet they don't really communicate with each other. I know this first hand because my wife and I used to have such a relationship.

On one occasion, my wife asked me to take her out to the movies, to which I gladly agreed. This seemed like a straightforward request with little room for miscommunication. However, at the time I had a major project deadline at work and I had a habit of coming home late. By the time I would get home from work, all the evening movies had already started. I didn't want to go to the late shows because I had to get up early the next morning. Also, I had to work on weekends to make up for time lost due to the constant interruptions I experienced at the office.

A week went by without us going to the movies, and by the second week, we had a fight. My wife was upset because I had promised to take her out to the movies and hadn't done so yet. I was upset because I felt she didn't make an effort to understand my situation at work, which was the reason I was coming home late every night.

Even though we had "talked" about going to the movies, we failed to "communicate" effectively.

THE THREE STAGES OF
EFFECTIVE COMMUNICATION

The reason my wife and I miscommunicated is that we used only two of the three stages of effective communication: *Talking* and *Listening,* but we missed the important last stage: *Feedback*.

STAGE 1: TALKING

When it comes to communicating effectively, talking is only the first step. Of all means of communication available to us (such as reading, writing, etc.) talking is the one we are most familiar with, which is not surprising since spoken language existed well before any form of written communication was ever created. Even in our own personal development, we learned to talk years before we learned to read and write.

However, this situation presents a problem: since talking comes so naturally to us, we tend to assume that we can communicate effectively just by talking to others. But talking alone isn't enough. When we communicate, information flows in two directions: outward and inward; whereas when we talk, information flows in only one direction: outward. To complete the cycle we need to move on to the second stage of effective communication: Listening.

STAGE 2: LISTENING

Listening provides us with the all-important return path in our communication cycle, however it encompasses much more than just hearing words. Much like our sense of sight, our sense of hearing is equally influenced by our "perception lens." As we learned in the chapter entitled *The Power of Perception,* what we see is not necessarily what's out there but an image "edited" by our beliefs. Similarly, what goes into our ears is not necessarily what we hear in our minds. In fact, our beliefs are subconsciously "editing" the content of what enters our field of hearing all the time.

When someone tells us something, we only hear what we perceive, which is not necessarily the message that was originally intended. The child's game "Broken Telephone" is a good illustration of this editing mechanism at work: one person whispers a message into the neighbor's ear and the message gets passed around the circle. The fun part happens when the last person in the circle tells the message to the group and it's usually significantly different from the original.

In essence, we listen selectively. What we are told and what we hear may not necessarily match. Consequently, our communication can easily break down unless we take steps to overcome this tendency. In order to do so, we have to take advantage of the third stage of effective communication.

STAGE 3: FEEDBACK

As we learned above, when we give others a message they will only listen to us selectively. Therefore, in order to ensure that our message gets across as intended, we have to verify that what they perceived in their minds actually matches what we meant to communicate. This is the nature of the feedback mechanism we have to establish.

Interestingly, most of the time we assume that if we know the person with whom we are communicating very well (e.g. a loved one), we can skip this third stage because we "think" we know how their minds work—therefore, we know how they will perceive and interpret our message. But this assumption is misleading because in many cases the people in our lives have beliefs that neither they nor we are aware of. As a result, we don't really know what it is they have actually perceived from our original message.

Let's analyze my earlier example about taking my wife to the movies in light of the above stages to see where our breakdown in communication took place.

Talking and Listening: My wife clearly told me that she wanted me to take her out to the movies, and I gladly agreed to do it.

The Hidden Belief: At the time, I was aware that it was going to be busy at work for the next few weeks because of my impending project deadline. However, I wasn't aware that I had the following belief: "Unless I am completely on top of my work, I am not allowed to have any fun time." So, when the words "I'd like you to take me to the movies" went into my ears, they got translated in my mind into "We'll go to the movies when everything at work is 100% under control."

As expected, things at work got progressively busier the closer I got to the project deadline. By the second week after my wife's original request, I was still promising I would take her out to the movies and yet I was continually coming home too late to fulfill my promise. *Consciously*, I had promised to take her out, but *subconsciously* I had made my promise conditional on some criteria my wife was never made aware of. With each broken promise, my wife's resentment and disappointment grew, as well as my own irritation that she wasn't being understanding of my situation.

The Breakdown: These pent-up feelings reared their ugly head in the second week when we had our fight. The fight was proof that we did not communicate effectively when we originally made our plans because both of us had different ideas about what we had agreed on. This was the breakdown in our communication.

Feedback: Since we never moved on to stage three (we both took the need for feedback for granted), my wife had no way of knowing that I was in no position to take her out to the movies until either my project was out of the way, or until I was able to change my belief about allowing myself to have fun time even when I am very busy at work.

Our breakdown could have been prevented very easily by soliciting feedback, such as by double-checking the original request. For example, after I consented to take her out my wife might have asked me if I was sure we could go to the movies given my busy schedule at work. This question would have given me a chance to take a second look at the strength of my commitment. I might have realized that I couldn't guarantee getting home early enough to catch a movie. As a result, I might have suggested an alternative, like getting a movie from the video store instead of going to the movie theater.

My alternative might not have fully satisfied my wife's original request, but it would have been much better than my repeated broken promises. Maybe she would have been open to it and maybe not. But if she wasn't, then this would have been an opportunity for us to communicate further in order to arrive at a solution that was satisfactory for both of us. Since we would have had a better understanding of what each of us wanted, an argument wouldn't have been our only means for resolution.

Many times, we are only open to hearing what we "want" to hear. My wife wanted to be taken out to the movies, so she wanted to hear "Yes, I'll take you out" in response to her request. The belief behind this expectation (as she told me later) was that if I didn't take her out on a date, symbolized by going to the movies, then that was a sign that I didn't care about her. Asking for feedback would have given me a chance to find out about her belief before getting into a confrontation. If I had known that her main preoccupation was that she wanted me to show that I cared, then I might have come up with a different alternative, like buying her flowers on the way home from work or giving her a thoughtful card.

WHY WE SKIP STAGES

The main reason we skip one or more of the stages of effective communication is that we tend to make a lot of assumptions. We assume everybody openly listens to what we say. We assume that everybody thinks exactly the way we think. We assume that if something makes sense to us then it must make sense to everybody else. And we make the greatest assumptions with those who are closest to us. The closer we are to someone, the more assumptions we make, and the more ineffective our communication turns out. We become "mind readers" of sorts and we start cutting corners on the three stages of effective communication.

When we assume, the first thing we typically do is to stop soliciting feedback. We think that we don't need to check what our partners have interpreted in their minds because we already know "how their minds work." Next, we stop listening. We assume that we already know what our partners are going to say, so we don't *really* listen to them. The last thing we do is to stop talking. Sometimes we assume that our partners can read our minds, so we only tell them part of the message and expect them to understand the whole of it. After all, if they are smart enough, they should be able to figure out the rest of the message on their own.

Assumptions cause us to bypass the three stages of effective communication.

The reason we assume so much is that it allows us to cut down on the time and effort required to communicate. We don't want to expend the extra energy because we don't think it's really necessary. *What we don't realize is that eventually it will take more time and effort to deal with the consequences of miscommunication than the time we save by cutting corners.*

Ultimately, effective communication can only happen at the mind level. In essence, when we communicate effectively, we are getting two different minds to agree on a common goal. By recognizing the role that our beliefs play in this process, and by using the three stages of effective communication with this knowledge in mind, we can significantly improve the quality of our relationships.

THE OPPOSITE RULES!

POPULAR RULE

As long as we talk and listen, we are communicating effectively.

OPPOSITE RULE

Talking and listening are only the beginning. Feedback is necessary to complete the cycle of effective communication.

EXPERIMENT:
GETTING FEEDBACK

This experiment encourages us to practice getting feedback when we communicate, as it is the most neglected of the three steps of effective communication.

- Choose an activity that you want to do with your partner, such as going out to the movies this week.

- First, decide for yourself when you would like to go, such as Friday at 7 PM.

- Next, ask your partner about it and be specific.

- If they agree to it, ask them to repeat back what they've understood, to make sure all the details are clear.

  If they repeat back what you think you communicated, you've achieved success. If they repeat something different, here's your chance to use feedback to its fullest. Maybe some negotiating is in order (like Friday is bad because she has aerobics class until 6:30 PM). But you've headed off a conflict because now you're both clear that another alternative must be chosen, which you wouldn't have known if you hadn't asked for feedback.

- Make a note of how the experiment worked for you. Did it help you understand your partner's perspective?

  _____

- Do you feel your partner understood your perspective more?

  _____

Getting feedback takes getting used to, but it is well worth the effort because it encourages mutual understanding in our relationships.

CHAPTER 2.4

DEALING WITH CRITICISM

All too often we have a lot of emotional "hot buttons" that are too easy for others to push. These buttons make us feel criticized and force us to be on the defensive. Imagine if we could change ourselves so that nothing people say about us would affect us negatively. That would be quite a treat, wouldn't it?

THE TRUTH ABOUT CRITICISM

When we react to a criticism, we are allowing somebody else's negative comments to affect the way we feel about ourselves. We let these negative comments hurt us because we have been conditioned over the years to give more importance to what other people think of us than to what *we* think of ourselves. On some level we believe that what others think of us is a reflection of who we are. The irony is that more often than not it is a reflection of who *they* are.

In fact, other people's criticisms have little to do with us and a lot to do with them. While this may be difficult to accept at first, consider that people can only make a criticism about something that resonates for them; in other words, something that they have beliefs about. In the chapter entitled *Our Belief System,* we learned that events or situations don't make us feel anything by themselves; it is our beliefs about those events or situations that trigger our emotions and cause us to make judgments. Consequently, any criticism directed towards us is nothing but a reflection of the beliefs of the person making the comment.

> *A criticism says more about the person*
> *making it than about the person receiving it.*

Knowing that criticisms from others say more about their own beliefs than they say about us can help us appease our reactions. We don't have to become so defensive. We can learn that we don't have to take things personally, and learn instead that our reactions are under nobody's control but our own. And as we become less reactive, we can seize the opportunity to find out what the real issue is behind the criticism.

Several years ago, I attended a personal growth seminar where we did an exercise on criticism. One participant, Joe, was paired up with another, Walter, whom for some reason Joe couldn't stand to be around. When asked why he was uncomfortable around him, Joe said that he couldn't tolerate people who smelled of cigarette smoke. To him, people who smoked were irresponsible and inconsiderate.

Now, that's quite the criticism! I imagine that when Joe revealed his opinion of smokers, Walter found it hard not to take it personally. However, since he was there to learn, he chose not to react to the comment. As well, since they had been complete strangers prior to this seminar, he was curious to find out how Joe could label him as irresponsible and inconsiderate when they had never met before. Joe didn't know him well enough to comment on whether or not he was a responsible and considerate person; all he knew was that he was a smoker.

When Joe was asked by the course facilitator if he wanted to explore his reaction to Walter, he said he did. He related that the cigarette smell on the other man's clothes reminded him of his father, who, in spite of his many pleas to quit smoking, remained a chain smoker until his premature death to lung cancer a few years back. Tears began coming down his face, as he confessed that he felt responsible for not having been able to save his father's life, whom he deeply loved. He realized that he was very angry at his father for having left him after he had begged him to quit, and that his own judgments about cigarette smokers were his way of dealing with his anger and pain.

It turned out that Joe's feelings about Walter were not about Walter at all, but about his own father and his inability to save him from his own demise. After Joe expressed his hurt and regret, he revealed that he felt much better and that he no longer "couldn't stand" Walter. On the contrary, he realized that Walter and his father had another similarity: they both had the same shape and color of eyes. Joe could now look at Walter and see someone he liked. As a matter of fact, he began to care for him by telling him that he really wished he'd quit smoking for his own good.

Walter admitted later on that at first he had felt slighted by Joe's initial comment, but had decided to hold off expressing his hurt until after Joe was done speaking. As Joe's story unfolded, Walter realized that Joe's criticism wasn't really about him, but a reflection of Joe's own pain. As a result, his feelings began to change. Instead of feeling slighted, he began to feel empathy. Because he decided not to indulge in feeling criticized, he allowed himself to be a part of another man's healing of a past hurt.

We can't control what others say to us or about us, but we can control how we respond to their comments. *We can choose how we respond to criticism and not let it affect our lives.* People may even purposely say words with the intent of hurting us, but we don't have to let our buttons be pushed. Granted, it would be great if we had no buttons to be pushed in the first place. In the meantime, we can try to understand that others have their own reasons for saying what they do and realize that we don't really have to be negatively affected by their comments.

We can choose how we respond to criticism.

Going back to the last example in the chapter entitled *The Power of Perception,* eleven-year-old Andrea didn't think at first that the word "tease" was offensive. It was only after her father told her that she should be angry about it that she began to take it personally. Up until then, the word had meant something different to her. The fact is that the comments Drew was making towards her said more about him than they did about Andrea. He was confused about his own sexual feelings for her and didn't know how to express them, so he chose to call her a "naughty" word. Had Andrea's father known that the comments others make reflect more about themselves than they do about the object of their comments, the whole situation would have unfolded differently. It's only when we *allow* our buttons to be pushed that we let other people's criticisms affect us.

OUR NEED FOR APPROVAL

We give so much importance to what other people think of us because most of us have been conditioned to believe that we must always present a good impression to those with whom we interact. We have a societal belief which states that "It's very important for others to like us"; therefore, we gauge how we are doing based on how others perceive us. If the feedback we receive (comments, opinions) is positive, then we must be on the right track. If it is negative (criticism, judgment), then we must have done something wrong.

Our dependence on the perception of others comes from our need for approval. When we feel we need approval, we place our focus on the feedback we feel we should get, instead of placing it on our own actions. Essentially, by looking for approval all we are really doing is making our self-esteem contingent on somebody else's assessment. As a result, when somebody makes a criticism about us we tend to take things personally because we feel that our self-esteem is on the line.

If we could somehow stop taking things personally, we would no longer be giving importance to what other people say about us. Imagine the freedom. We could do what we wanted without fear that other people's words might have the power to bring us down. People's criticisms would be no different to us than their comments about the weather. Since we'd be taking their words for what they are, just their own opinion, we wouldn't feel like we had to take offense if we didn't agree with them.

Since everybody is entitled to their own beliefs, everybody is by extension entitled to their own opinion. Essentially, nobody's opinion is better or worse than anybody else's. We only react to them when *we* personalize them. There's no reason why we should hold someone else's opinion higher than our own if that opinion will end up hurting the way we feel about ourselves.

This doesn't mean, however, that we should disregard all opinions that come our way. They could contain valuable information that might indeed help us, which is the point of "constructive criticism." However, we must always keep in mind that all opinions are just a representation of somebody else's point of view and not a commentary on our adequacy or inadequacy as a person.

Sometimes, what we perceive to be a criticism may not have even been intended as such. I was once attending a speech class where the teacher was explaining the differences in the placement of the tongue for various European languages. He was commenting on how the texture of British English is very precise while the texture of French is more loose and has a sensual feel to it. Then, he explained that Hungarian is a very interesting language because it incorporates elements of texture from both British English and French. He proceeded to say a few words in Hungarian to demonstrate this phenomenon.

As I was listening to the demonstration, I could clearly hear how the Hungarian accent combined the precision of British English with the sensuality of French. So I shared my observation with the class. Almost immediately, a British woman sitting next to me jumped to her feet and, sounding very offended, demanded to know if I was implying that British people aren't sensual! This woman heard a criticism even though none was intended. Nevertheless, I apologized for the misunderstanding, since it hadn't been my intention to offend her. Sometimes what we think is a criticism might not even be one at all!

CRITICISM IN OUR RELATIONSHIPS

If we allow the words of a stranger to affect our self-esteem so deeply, it's no wonder that our personal relationships become a playing ground for power games and manipulation. When we are in a relationship, we develop an emotional attachment with our partner. When we take what they say personally, we are letting this attachment take control over our self-esteem. By taking their comments personally, we are subconsciously putting them in charge of our emotional hot buttons.

However, by developing our own internal reference point, as explained in the chapter entitled *Good News and Bad News,* we can make our self-esteem independent of this emotional attachment thereby making our hot buttons lose their power. What's fascinating about this process is that as soon as our buttons become ineffective, our partners slowly stop making hurtful comments to us. The reason their negative comments become less frequent is that as they begin to realize that they are no longer in charge of our buttons, they start to subconsciously shift their own behavior in order to adapt to the new reality they now find themselves in.

This subconscious process is known as *mirroring* and we will discuss it in detail in the upcoming chapter entitled *The Law of Attraction*. But let's briefly explain what's behind this process. In any relationship, the behavior of both partners is linked. Even though people's behaviors are a reflection of their own beliefs, the primary reason people are together in a relationship is that their beliefs are compatible. For instance, if Mark is a critical person and his wife Joan is insecure, there is a natural reason why they are together in a relationship. Critical people subconsciously look for insecure people to criticize, and conversely, insecure people subconsciously look for critical people to feed their insecurity.

But when one of the partners begins a process of change, the other partner feels a void that can only be filled by adapting to the new reality, so that their beliefs can go back to being compatible again. For instance, if Joan starts becoming more secure and assertive, then Mark's criticisms will no longer work because they will not elicit the same reaction as before. Because the rules of relating have changed, Mark will start shifting his behavior subconsciously to match Joan's new behavior.

Of course, it should be noted that, oftentimes, there is a period of transition when one person starts changing. As Joan starts becoming more assertive and less insecure, Mark might respond by becoming even more critical because he is not used to this behavior. Since there's been a shift in the way they both interact and the old strategies Mark had for getting what he wanted aren't working, he is subconsciously trying to get the relationship back to "normal." So he criticizes more. Even though he might like Joan's new assertiveness on a conscious level, he finds her new behavior threatening on a subconscious level because it involves making a change he wasn't expecting to make. What's important to remember is that this is only a transitional phase: Joan is becoming more assertive and Mark is trying to adjust to the change. She may feel a bit uncertain at times during this phase because the rules are changing for her as well. But if Joan keeps persisting in trying to be less insecure and more assertive, eventually Mark will become less critical because his criticisms won't be having the effect they used to. In essence, the mirror will have changed.

Having our relationships change for the better is one of the most significant benefits of learning how to become immune to criticism.

Once we develop this skill in our lives, we'll be taking our relationships to higher levels of enjoyment and understanding.

LEAVING CRITICISM BEHIND

When we rely so heavily on what other people think of us, we end up going through cycles of low self-esteem and high self-esteem. One day we may get a nice comment and our self-esteem goes up. The next day, we may hear a criticism and it goes back down. We move forward three steps and then go back two. Therefore, we end up progressing in our lives at a much slower rate than we are really capable of.

We can disarm our tendency to take things personally by continuing to develop our own internal reference point. If we can learn to measure our growth based on how *we* feel we are progressing, then we will become immune to what other people think of us. Of course, people will still make comments about us. Some will appear to be positive, and some will appear to be negative; however, these comments won't have the same impact on our self-esteem as before because we'll no longer be allowing our emotions to depend on the words of others to determine how we feel. Once we make our self-esteem independent of external circumstances, we can grow at a much faster rate because we are not stopping our growth in reaction to somebody else's comment, opinion, or perception of us.

> *An internal reference point helps*
> *us become immune to criticism.*

We can use our internal reference point to reverse our propensity to allow others to evaluate our worth. By making our self-esteem independent of external factors, we can take on all the forward steps we want without having to worry about taking any steps backward (to learn how to develop your own internal reference point, refer to the experiment at the end of the chapter entitled *Good News and Bad News*.)

As we start noticing that the comments and criticisms of other people reflect their own beliefs and opinions, it will become easier for us to be less reactive to their words. We'll know that they are entitled to believe whatever they want but that their comments don't have to impact how we feel about ourselves. In knowing that we can choose how we respond to the opinions of others, we can begin to let go of needing their approval. Beginning to develop and use our own reference point will help make us depend less on what others think of us and more on what we think about ourselves. As a result, our relationships will only become healthier since our self-esteem will no longer be hostage to other people's opinions.

THE OPPOSITE RULES!

POPULAR RULE

A criticism must reflect an unfavorable aspect of ourselves, otherwise we would not have been criticized in the first place.

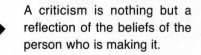

OPPOSITE RULE

A criticism is nothing but a reflection of the beliefs of the person who is making it.

EXPERIMENT:
HANDLING CRITICISM

The goal of this experiment is to start becoming aware of how we react to criticism.

• Think of a criticism someone said to you this week that you felt hurt by (e.g. "What's with the silly haircut?"). Write it below:

_____

_____

• Write your feelings here as a result of the criticism. (e.g. angry, embarrassed, hurt, regretful)

_____

• Now, think back to how you felt about the thing being criticized *before* the criticism was made (e.g. excited about your new "look" or disappointed in the way it turned out).

_____

• If you originally felt positive about it, why did you allow your feelings to change as a result of their comment?

_____

• If you didn't like it, then in fact you agree with the criticism on some level. (e.g. you might believe that you "should have" kept the previous style). Even if you feel they're "right," why do you think you have to feel bad about it?

_____

• If you have uncovered a limiting belief as a result of this experiment, write it below:

_____

_____

Chapter 2.5
When We Become Judge and Jury

In the same way that we fall victim to criticism from time to time, we often become the makers of judgments ourselves. Whether we do it as part of an argument or as a passing comment, and whether we do it in person or behind someone's back, many of us spend a significant part of our lives making judgments about other people. We make judgments about their choices, their circumstances, their behavior, their opinions, the events taking place in their lives, and so on. These people might be our loved ones, relatives, friends, acquaintances or even total strangers. In all cases, when we witness or hear of something involving someone else, we often feel the urge to provide our critical viewpoint.

While most times our judgments may appear to be nothing but innocent passing comments, in reality they can cause a lot of harm to our personal growth. Whenever we make negative comments about other people, we relegate ourselves to the position of passive commentators who stand on the sidelines. Instead of being active participants in our own lives, we become "repeater stations" of someone else's experiences. When we are so focused on the happenings in the lives of others, we are not focusing on our own lives. As a result, our personal growth suffers.

If we look around us, we might discover that the people who judge the most are those who don't seem to be very happy in their lives, while those who judge the least are often people who are relatively satisfied with how their lives are going. Essentially, when we focus on what we can do for ourselves in order to pursue our goals, then we are too busy to concern ourselves with what Mark or Jim or Susan or Bob or Angela are doing. The less we judge others, the more we can focus on our own growth.

TWO COMMON TYPES OF JUDGMENT

There are two common types of judgment people tend to use the most: the judgment of someone else's choices and the judgment of the person (or personal attack).

The *judgment of someone's choices* is a type of judgment that is used when we have a limited view of the world and its possibilities; in other words, our own beliefs about the possibilities that exist out there are too restrictive. When we have this limited view, we have the urge to discredit anything that challenges our beliefs of what's possible. Some examples of judgment of someone's choices are: "How could she possibly make a living as an artist?" or "Where does he get the audacity to wear those clothes?" or "She's wasting a lot of money on her fancy trips." Essentially, all these comments reflect the limiting beliefs of whoever is making them. The first statement reflects a disbelief toward someone making a living in a creative field, the second one reflects a restricted fashion consciousness of what's acceptable, while the third reflects the belief that money shouldn't be wasted on trips. These judgments criticize the actions made by others and reflect the disbelief that anyone could make such choices. In summary, when we judge someone's choices, all we are doing is making comments that reflect what *we* believe to be possible in the world.

The *personal judgment* or *personal attack,* on the other hand, is used when limiting beliefs we have about *ourselves* are challenged by the actions of others. These are more personal because they touch on something we feel deeply about ourselves, but perhaps don't want to acknowledge. We may have wanted what other people have achieved, but since we never believed that we could do it, we feel we have to put them down in order to artificially prop up our self-esteem. We try to "excuse" their success by discrediting them in some way. As a result, our comments take on a very personal nature in order to make ourselves somewhat superior. Some examples of personal attack are: "He's not talented enough to deserve all that money,"

"She's too ugly to be a model," and "He's not good enough to be on this team." While the comments appear to be about someone else, they really are a reflection of the beliefs that we hold about ourselves. On some level, we believe that we are "not talented enough" or "too ugly" or "not good enough," but we project these beliefs onto someone else.

---

*Our judgments speak more about us
than about the people we are judging.*

Whether we judge people's choices or judge them personally, we are automatically reacting to the perception that our beliefs are being challenged. It is our own perception that triggers our judgments, not the actions of the people we are judging. As we learned in the previous chapter, a criticism says more about the person making it than about the person receiving it. Essentially, what we are dealing with here is the flip side of the same coin, since when we judge others, our comments reveal a lot about our own insecurities and limiting beliefs.

JUDGMENTS IN OUR RELATIONSHIPS

When Tom's nineteen-year-old son Josh told him that he was planning to quit college to start a rock band with three of his friends, he panicked and became very angry. He told Josh that quitting school would be the worst thing he could do for himself and that he would regret this decision for the rest of his life. Tom further threatened that if he quit school to start a rock band, he would no longer support him financially, which meant that Josh wouldn't be able to fend for himself. Further, he warned that when he failed (this being just a matter of time), he wouldn't have an education to fall back on since he would have quit the only thing that could give him a future. Finally, Tom told his son that he should put some distance between him and his "musician" friends until he gets over the nonsense of becoming a rock star, and that sticking to the family tradition of getting a college education would be the best thing for him to do.

Josh was completely shocked at his father's harsh and critical reaction. He immediately felt very defensive and countered angrily to Tom that he'd been extremely unfair with him. He told him that he was wrong to think that he and his friends aren't good enough musicians to succeed. When his father didn't respond, he yelled that college is too boring for him and that he doesn't want to spend his time learning things he knows he'll never use. He then accused Tom of being too old and uptight to understand and that he was wasting his time in trying to tell him what to do. Josh then added that he is old enough to do whatever he wants with his life and that he didn't need his father's narrow-minded opinion anyway. Finally, he stormed out of the room.

This confrontation left both Tom and Josh extremely upset and confused. Although they both started out wanting to have a constructive discussion about Josh's plans, they ended up judging each other to the point that neither of them wanted to listen anymore. As a result, they both left the argument with bad feelings about each other and themselves. Tom was angry at his son for wanting to quit college and at himself for not getting Josh to understand his reasons. Josh, on the other hand, was sorry he even tried to talk to his old-fashioned father to begin with.

Because they spent their time together making judgments, they never got the chance to understand each other's side. Both of them had valid points to make, but the problems began when they expressed their views in the form of a judgment. Tom's comments that quitting school was the worst thing Josh could do to himself, that Josh wouldn't be able to fend for himself, that wanting to be a rock star was nonsense, and that college was the best thing for him, were judgments that questioned Josh's intelligence and ability to figure out what is good for him. Josh ended up feeling unsupported, criticized, belittled and angry. Conversely, Josh's comments that Tom was wrong, that he was too old and uptight to understand, and that he was narrow-minded, were judgments that questioned Tom's ability to be of help and to be supportive. As a result of these comments, Tom ended up feeling even angrier and more resentful of his son. Because they judged each other, they put themselves in their least resourceful state possible for having a constructive discussion about Josh's career.

Using judgments as a means of communicating can only close off the lines of communication.

Let's try to uncover the true source of these judgments by taking a behind-the-scenes look at Tom and Josh's argument. The reason why Tom felt so strongly that his son Josh was making a mistake wasn't based on some statistics he had come across showing the failure rate of young adults quitting school to start rock bands. On the contrary, a good number of rock bands started out this way and eventually became very successful. Tom's reaction wasn't based on his own life experience either, since he had never done anything like it. The only reason why Tom reacted so strongly to his son's news was that **it seriously challenged his own beliefs.**

Therefore, in order to analyze Tom's reaction, we first have to take a look at his beliefs. He believes that having an education must be first and foremost in a person's life. He also believes that a person can only make a living with a solid and "safe" profession (certainly not as a rock musician). Tom reacted negatively to his son's plans because his own *beliefs* could not conceive of anyone making a living by playing in a rock band. In essence, he was making a judgment about his son's choices. The above beliefs are some of the ones which form Tom's perception of what's right and wrong. *It is this perception that was at the core of Tom's extreme reaction and that prompted him to judge his son.*

Because Tom took his son's news as a challenge to his own beliefs, he wasn't in the best frame of mind to support him. All Josh really wanted was to get some feedback on his ideas to start a rock band, but what he got instead were a barrage of judgments. Feeling hurt and angry for being judged for the choices he wanted to make, Josh immediately began to personally attack his father. He criticized him for being too old and narrow-minded to understand. Josh's response was intense because he felt that *his own* beliefs were being challenged. His beliefs about his own ability to know what's best for himself were called into question, and because he was at a turning point in his life, having these beliefs questioned put his sense of self at risk. The conflict between the two men escalated to the point where both sets of beliefs were so severely threatened by the judgments each were making, that the argument had to end without a resolution.

Making judgments is our way of protecting our beliefs when we feel they are being challenged.

As we've seen in Tom and Josh's example, judgments don't help us find a common ground; on the contrary, they often drive us apart. Instead of being open to listening to or accepting other people and recognizing that they have different beliefs than ours, we end up reacting as if our own beliefs are being called into question. What this does is create a wedge of distance between us because we are no longer trying to *understand the other person,* but are instead trying to *defend our beliefs.* No longer about the issue at hand, the conflict becomes a battle of wills—whose belief can "win" the battle.

Recognizing that our beliefs are at the root of our judgments is the first step towards becoming less judgmental. As we move towards becoming less critical of others, we'll be able to communicate better with the people in our lives.

DEVELOPING THE HABIT OF NONJUDGMENT

How do we go about becoming less judgmental? We can begin by trying the following simple technique to defuse our judgments. Whenever you feel that you are about to judge somebody, try to think of something positive you know about this person. In doing so, you are taking your attention away from your challenged beliefs; as a result, they won't be threatened as much.

Let's go back to Tom and Josh's confrontation to see how Tom could have applied this technique to better handle his son's news. When Josh told Tom of his plan to quit college to start a rock band, Tom had a strong urge to tell him that he was making a big mistake. If he had been able to stop himself from making this unsupportive comment to Josh and instead had focused on the fact that his son is a smart person (this is something good about Josh that doesn't challenge Tom's beliefs), he would have given him the opportunity to explain his rationale for his plan to start a rock band.

While this shift in focus wouldn't have necessarily eliminated Tom's limiting belief about rock bands, at least it would have given his son the benefit of the doubt and possibly head off the argument. By holding off his judgment and focusing on a positive aspect about Josh, Tom could have listened to his son and helped him find his own answers. They could have had a good talk about it and together they could have found the best solution for Josh.

The more we catch ourselves when we are about to judge someone and replace our criticism with a positive thought, the more comfortable we'll become with the practice of nonjudgment in our lives. We'll begin to feel freer because we will be chipping away at the power our limiting beliefs have over us. As well, becoming nonjudgmental will also be beneficial for our psychological health because we'll get caught up less and less in the exhausting emotions of reacting to others and defending our limiting beliefs.

By developing the habit of nonjudgment, we'll naturally have a more relaxed approach to life. Instead of getting into made-up fights that don't add any value to our lives, we will be free to resume our path of growth, and in turn allow others to resume theirs.

THE OPPOSITE RULES!

POPULAR RULE

Our judgments are comments about someone else's inadequacies.

➡

OPPOSITE RULE

Our judgments reveal more about ourselves than about the people we are judging.

EXPERIMENT:
BEING LESS JUDGMENTAL

The goal of this experiment is to become aware of your judgments and how they reflect aspects of yourself.

• Write down a judgment you made about someone's choices:

_____

• Write down a personal judgment you made:

_____

These judgments reveal hidden beliefs you have about yourself.

• Think about what the possible beliefs are for both of the judgments, and write them below:

_____

_____

_____

_____

What these judgments may indicate is a regret about the past or a wish for the future. Perhaps you want to try something that someone else tried but don't have the courage yet. Take heart that knowing why you make certain judgments can lead you to discovering what you truly want for yourself.

Chapter 2.6
The Art of Peace

Achieving lasting peace in our relationships can sometimes feel impossible. There always seems to be something negative happening with the people in our lives, such as criticism, manipulation, or conflicts of one kind or another. While on occasion we do experience moments of bliss, oftentimes it feels like an uphill battle just to get our partner to support us and to nurture us. Let's now look at effective ways to reinvent our relationships so that we can truly achieve lasting peace with the people in our lives as well as with ourselves.

Living with Different Belief Systems

By now, we are very much aware of the major influence that our beliefs have on the way we behave, feel, and perceive the world around us. We also know that everybody is different because no two people have exactly the same beliefs. If we did, we would all appear to be the same, down to the way we think, the way we feel, the way we behave, and the circumstances surrounding us. Whenever we enter into a relationship, we suddenly have two different sets of beliefs sharing a common experience. Since everybody has their own personal definition of right and wrong according to their own beliefs, behaviors that may be perfectly acceptable for one individual, may be offensive to the other. For example, there are cultures in the world were one shows appreciation to the host at the end of a meal by burping at the table, yet in North American society this is considered offensive.

Within a relationship, the differences between partners may not be as marked as in the above example, but even at more subtle levels, they are always present. For instance, Martha believes that everything has a place and everything must be in its place. She acquired this belief because when she was growing up, her house was always a mess and she could never find what she was looking for. As an adult, she decides that in her house, everything will be kept neatly in place. Having everything in place gives her the sense of stability she felt she missed out on earlier in her life.

On the other hand, Sam, her partner, believes that having everything in its place is restrictive to his freedom because when he was a child his parents had very rigid rules about where things go in the house. As a result, now that he's an adult and doesn't live at home anymore, he wants to experience the freedom of living his life without any restrictions. Having a few things strewn about make him feel relaxed.

In their own minds, Martha and Sam are doing what's right for themselves, but it happens to be what's wrong for the other person. They both have conflicting beliefs, and as a result they have conflict in their lives. In order to move past this conflict and into a resolution, they first need to acknowledge and accept their inherent differences.

THE HEALING POWER OF THE APOLOGY

Our ability to resolve our conflicting beliefs centers around the effective use of the apology. Unfortunately, there is a misconception about apologizing. It's common to think that by saying "I'm sorry" we are saying "You were right and I was wrong." We feel that if we apologize, we are implicitly admitting defeat.

However, apologizing isn't about being right or wrong. Instead, it is a clue as to how our beliefs are different. For instance, in the earlier story about the speech class I attended, I apologized to the British woman who was offended by my comment in class not because she was "right" and I was "wrong," but as a way of acknowledging that what I said hurt her feelings. Even though my comment harbored no ill intent, her beliefs about what I said made it wrong to *her*. By making an apology, I wasn't taking responsibility for the way she felt, since only she can be responsible for her own feelings. Instead, I was expressing *my acknowledgment* that her beliefs were different from mine. My apology proved to her that I was making an effort to heal a conflict of beliefs.

Acknowledging our difference in beliefs through the use of the apology opens the door to finding a resolution for the conflicts in our relationships. What often happens in a conflict is that we stop communicating because we are angry. An apology can heal some of the anger so that we can get back to communicating effectively.

If we refuse to apologize to our partners and remain hardheaded about what we said or did, then we are telling them that we aren't willing to accept that they have different beliefs than us. In fact, we are telling them that their beliefs are wrong. And as we already know, if they feel their beliefs are being challenged, their sense of self will feel challenged as well. The result is that the conflict will escalate as our partners fight to defend their beliefs instead of focusing on the root of the conflict itself. By refusing to apologize, we are, in effect, letting our pride get in the way of gaining a better understanding about our relationship.

Apologizing opens the door to understanding.

How do we take advantage of the power of the apology without feeling that we are losing out? By realizing that saying "I'm sorry" is not an acknowledgment on our part that our beliefs are "wrong," but a recognition that our partner is entitled to have different beliefs than we do. In essence, **apologizing is not about acknowledging fault, but about accepting differences.** Incidentally, this recognition does not imply that we have to agree with our partner's beliefs. It simply means that we are accepting that their beliefs don't necessarily have to match ours.

Knowing that an apology can simply be an acknowledgment of differing beliefs and not an admission of failure can be very freeing for us. No longer are our beliefs wrong; they are simply different. This knowledge also places us in a non confrontational frame of mind. When our partners feel hurt by something we did or said, we are free to open the door to healing by saying "I'm sorry what I said or did hurt you." Quite often, we'll discover that the apology is all our partners were looking for. On a subconscious level, whatever we said or did that hurt them challenged one of their deeply held beliefs. As a result, all they wanted was an apology to affirm that their beliefs are OK.

Saying "I'm sorry" when we are not used to apologizing may feel a bit uncomfortable at first (the old pride is sometimes hard to let go of). But learning to apologize as our way of acknowledging the differences in our beliefs can lead to wonderful benefits in our relationships.

GIVING THE GIFT OF APPRECIATION

While apologizing can be of great help in healing our relationship conflicts, an excellent way of lowering the number of conflicts in the first place is to develop the habit of appreciation.

One of the most common sources of ill feelings in relationships is being taken for granted. There are two main reasons why we take our partners for granted. First, the longer we are in a relationship, the more complacent we tend to become. We feel that we don't have to acknowledge our partners' contribution as much because we have come to "expect" it. Second, if we have done something nice for our partners, then we may feel as if they "owe" us. So when they do something nice for us later on, we feel we don't have to show any appreciation for it because we think that they are simply paying us back for what we did for them earlier.

Although taking partners for granted is quite common in relationships, it results in a major problem: *it generates strong feelings of resentment*. Unfortunately resentment is one of those feelings that we can't easily vent, unlike anger or frustration. In addition to eroding our relationships, resentment festers in our bodies and, if not dealt with, it can lead to health problems. As a matter of fact, if bottled up long enough these health problems can become quite serious, as alluded to earlier in the story about the concert violinist who gave up her promising career when she married the military career officer *(The Manipulationship)*.

The best antidote against the buildup of resentment in our relationships is to start appreciating the little things our partners do for us. A simple "Thank you" is enough to begin with. The next step is to develop the habit of appreciation in our lives. By acknowledging our partner every time they put some effort into the relationship, we are encouraging them to strengthen their commitment to it. Our appreciation will make them feel loved and cherished. It will make them feel that all the effort they are putting into our relationship is well worth it.

Once we start being more appreciative of the things our partners do for us every day, we'll discover that appreciation breeds appreciation. When our partners feel appreciated, they will start thanking us for our own contributions. Instead of having a chain reaction of negativity, we'll experience a snow ball effect of harmony. Resentment will slowly be replaced by pleasure. And interestingly, there is no effort involved in this transformation. All it takes is to put our expectations and pride aside, and every now and then utter two simple words: *Thank You*.

Being appreciative is the best antidote for resentment.

Everybody has a good side and a bad side. The key to fulfilling relationships is to bring out the best in people as much as we can. And the easiest way of achieving this goal is to show appreciation for the contributions they make in our lives.

TOWARDS A GUILT-FREE RELATIONSHIP

The last step towards achieving a lasting sense of peace in our relationships is to curb the use of guilt as a motivator for giving and receiving. For instance, if somebody gives you a gift, do you feel you owe him or her to reciprocate it?

Giving out of owing is the weakest form of giving because it's based on guilt instead of sincerity. Guilt-based giving is not very healthy for our relationships, since guilt is one of the most limiting and harmful feelings around. It takes away the freedom to give and makes giving a "should." The reason most of us are hooked on guilt is that it's a very effective manipulation technique in our society. As we discussed earlier in the chapter entitled *The Manipulationship*, we learned how to manipulate others at a very young age so that we could get what we wanted out of them.

If we feel we "owe" something to somebody, then we are allowing ourselves to become victims of a subtle form of manipulation. Whether somebody is consciously trying to manipulate us or not is inconsequential. The minute we "owe" someone, our relationship with that person suffers. If we say "You shouldn't have" when someone gives us a gift, we are essentially trying to get rid of the feeling that we "have to" give them something in return. Because they shouldn't have, we don't have to. This is just a way of alleviating our guilt and hoping that they won't be keeping score because now it's our turn. Feeling that we owe someone takes away our freedom to do what we really want to do.

A story comes to mind from a seminar I once attended with my wife. As we were checking into our hotel room the night before the seminar, we were pleasantly surprised to find a beautiful basket with fruit, candy, cookies, and top quality Swiss chocolates waiting for us. Along with the basket came a note from Sean, the learning center's head of development, welcoming us back as we had attended several other courses there in the past. Naturally, the first chance we had to see him, we thanked him for his generous gift.

A couple of days into the seminar, we were invited to participate in a presentation that Sean was going to give after class about new activities that were coming up at the center. Unfortunately, the date of the presentation coincided with my wife's birthday and I was planning to take her out for a romantic dinner.

I suddenly found myself torn. I wanted to take my wife out to dinner, but at the same time, I felt that I "should" attend this presentation because of the beautiful basket we were given. I felt fearful about making either decision. I was afraid that if I went to this presentation out of guilt, I was going to feel miserable for postponing the birthday celebration that I had planned for my wife. If, on the other hand, I took her out to a romantic restaurant, I feared I wouldn't be able to enjoy the evening because I would feel tormented for having "betrayed" Sean's generosity. For most of that day, I felt tense and out of sorts because I didn't want to make a decision one way or the other.

The way I saw it, either decision would have been wrong because, in my mind, I couldn't please both my wife *and* Sean. If I went to the presentation, then I felt that my relationship with my wife would suffer (whether she was aware of my feeling or not). If I went to the romantic dinner, then I felt that my relationship with Sean would suffer (again, whether he was aware of my feeling or not).

Fortunately, my wonderful wife sensed my paralysis and came to my rescue. She made me realize that neither did I "owe" her a birthday dinner nor did I "owe" Sean my presence at his presentation. If I wanted to go to one or the other I would have to do it because I wanted to and not because I "owed" it to anyone.

After thinking about what she said, I realized that what I *really* wanted to do was to take her out for her birthday dinner since it had been my original plan. On the other hand, I had never planned to attend the center's presentation, since I only found out about it after we arrived there. My choice was now clear. We went to our romantic dinner and had a fabulous time together. No feeling of guilt or betrayal towards Sean ever came up during the meal and my relationship with my wife became stronger as a result.

By allowing guilt into our lives, we are putting ourselves in a position where we are damned if we do and damned if we don't. **Doing something out of owing is restrictive and crippling, whereas doing something out of wanting is very freeing and fulfilling.**

Learning to give freely because *we want to* helps us learn how to receive as well. "Receiving" means that we are freely accepting something that someone has given us, and not feeling that we have to reciprocate. All that is required is a simple "Thank you."

When we learn how to give and receive without guilt, our relationships become that much more fulfilling. No longer are we doing things because *we have to* or in return for something given to us, but instead because we feel good giving something to someone we care about. As well, when we feel good about giving, we also learn to receive more freely. Since we know that the other person doesn't "owe" us anything and has exercised their choice to give us something, we no longer feel guilty about receiving it.

Next time you feel you have to do or reciprocate something, consider if you are doing it out of guilt or out of wanting. If it is out of guilt, try to understand why you feel guilty. Is it because you feel that you are not doing enough in the relationship, or maybe you feel you "should" since they have given you something earlier? If you can figure out the reason why you feel you *have to,* then you can look at how you might want to change that. You can try to experiment with giving out of wanting instead, or if that is too much right now, then it's probably a good idea not to reciprocate; you may have a belief about guilt that needs to be looked at before you can give freely.

It's important not to worry about consequences when you're learning how to give out of wanting. No matter what you do, you will *always* be worse off by doing things out of guilt because you'll be perpetuating the "owing" nature of the relationship. Moreover, giving repeatedly out of guilt encourages the recipients to take you for granted. This happens because you are subconsciously suggesting that the reason you are giving them something is that you think you owe them, not because you care about them.

Try guilt-free giving in your relationships and look at them reach new levels of appreciation. And don't expect anything in return. If you do, you may be inadvertently encouraging people to owe you! Learn to give simply because you *want* to. The appreciation you will receive is the best gift you can get in return.

THE OPPOSITE RULES!

POPULAR RULE

When we apologize, we are implicitly admitting defeat.

OPPOSITE RULE

An apology is just an acknowledgment that people have different beliefs.

When someone gives us something, then we owe them something in return.

When somebody gives us something, we don't *owe* them anything in return. If we decide to give, though, it is much more fulfilling to do so because we *want to* than because we *have to*.

EXPERIMENT:
GUILT-FREE GIVING

This experiment gives us an opportunity to practice giving when "we want to" instead of giving when we feel we "have to." Giving doesn't always have to involve a present, although that's how we are programmed in society. A gift can also be time spent with someone, or a compliment, or simply saying "I love you." We can relearn how to give without feeling guilty and once we practice a few times, we'll see how good and rewarding our lives begin to feel.

- Think of some things you may want to give to someone in your life: fresh-cut flowers to your wife for "no reason," some time spent with your younger sister. List three of them below:

  1 _____

  2 _____

  3 _____

- Pick one of these things and give it this week. Give freely and with a smile. If the other person says, "Oh you shouldn't have!," just smile and say, "I was thinking of you and really wanted to give it to you. I hope you enjoy it."

- Try to experiment regularly with "giving because you simply want to" without expecting anything in return. In time, you may be surprised to find your relationships becoming more and more authentic.

CHAPTER 2.7
THE LAW OF ATTRACTION

It is remarkable how many patterns from our childhood we unknowingly repeat in our adult relationships. For instance, how many women do we know that marry men who exhibit the same behaviors their fathers had towards their mothers? How many men do we know that marry women who treat them like their mothers treated their fathers? We don't have to look too far to find such cases. We can see them in our friendships, in our families, perhaps even in our own relationships.

In this chapter, we are going to look at why we attract people into our lives and what we can do to attract the kind of people we *really* want to have around.

HOW THE LAW OF ATTRACTION WORKS

One of the big ironies of life is that in spite of promising ourselves that we'll never "become our parents," we often end up repeating many of their patterns of behavior in our own adult relationships. The reason for this ironic twist is that even though we might be aware of specific behavioral patterns from home that we don't want to repeat, most times we aren't aware of the underlying beliefs that are triggering those behaviors in the first place. Since our behavior is a reflection of our beliefs, any relationship belief that we have inherited from our upbringing (whether it is a limiting one or an empowering one) will manifest itself as a behavior in our adult lives, whether we want it to or not.

What is puzzling, however, is how we manage to draw into our lives total strangers who have the mysterious talent of matching these patterns perfectly. The solution to this puzzle lies in of one of the most powerful and yet least talked about aspects of human relationships: *The Law of Attraction* (sometimes referred to as "mirroring"). Basically, this law states the following:

We only attract into our lives people who fulfill our beliefs and whose beliefs we fulfill ourselves.

Whenever we interact with others, we only attract those people who find what we say and do (i.e. our behavior) appealing. Since our behavior is nothing but a reflection of our beliefs, those people we attract into our lives are ultimately attracted to our beliefs. And the reason they are attracted to them is that *our beliefs happen to fulfill the needs of their own beliefs*. That's how relationships work. If there are no beliefs being mutually fulfilled, then there is no relationship. When people say, "You can tell a lot about people by the friends they have," what they're really saying is that our friends are an outward representation of what we believe inside. In essence, the people we choose to relate to are people who have beliefs that complement ours.

What makes a belief complementary is that both people in the relationship have beliefs that work well together, although "working well together" doesn't always mean that everything is OK in the relationship. For example, if we have a belief that states that "In order to be loved I have to be a victim," then we'll attract people into our lives who fulfill our belief by victimizing us. As a result, we might have partners who are bossy or may blame us for anything that doesn't go their way. Their behavior supports our belief that we have to be a victim so that we can get love. Mind you, at a conscious level we may hate their behavior, but subconsciously, we are getting exactly what we want them to provide us with. Interestingly, by hating their behavior we are reinforcing our role of victim even more because the more we acknowledge being bossed around (through complaining and hating), the more we strengthen our sense of victimization.

The law of attraction works equally for our partner. In the same way that our partner fulfills our beliefs, we fulfill theirs. For instance, a partner who has the above traits might have a belief that states that "For me to love you, you always have to do as I say." A victim is the perfect match for someone with this type of belief. Again, our partner may consciously hate our own behavior and think that we are weak and whiny, but subconsciously, this is exactly the way they want us to behave. As well, their contempt for our behavior will result in even more abuse, thus reinforcing their role as victimizer.

THE LAW OF ATTRACTION AND CHILDREN

The law of attraction is not only restricted to our relationship with our partners. It works equally well with our families, coworkers, friendships, even our children.

When it comes to children, we obviously don't attract them to our lives; we conceive them. However, the behaviors they exhibit while they are growing up are more than likely to be what we subconsciously need in order to fulfill our own beliefs. *In essence, our children develop the complementary beliefs that are necessary to fulfill our own.*

A friend of mine has had an interesting experience with the *Law of Attraction* and her five-year-old child. My friend grew up in South America and moved to the United States when her husband was transferred by his company. Even though she had learned English for many years back home, when they moved to the United States she didn't feel comfortable with her command of the language. She had the belief that since she had been raised speaking a different language, she would never be able to be perfectly fluent in a second language.

As a result of this belief, whenever she had to express a thought in English, her mind would become clouded and the right words just wouldn't come out of her mouth. She knew very well how to put those words together, but her belief made her lose confidence in herself. This is the way our beliefs work—as long as we believe them to be true, then we bring them to life through our behavior.

The most interesting part was that her American-born child had developed the same confidence problem *she* had even though he was born into an English culture, with English TV shows, books, music, teachers, friends, and so on. His difficulties with the English language developed because he was reflecting, or "mirroring," his mom's limiting belief (this is why the law of attraction is also referred to as "mirroring"). In essence, his behavior had to mirror his mom's belief about having trouble speaking a second language, since fulfilling this belief kept him close to her.

THE SWITCHING PHENOMENON

An interesting side-effect of the law of attraction takes place when one person in a relationship stops exhibiting the behavior they've always had and adopts instead the behavior of the other person. Surprisingly, the other person automatically switches and starts exhibiting the behavior of the first person! This is a pattern that my wife has come to label as "The Switching Phenomenon," which is something I have experienced firsthand with her. Understanding how this phenomenon works can be useful in helping partners become more aware of the limiting beliefs they mirror for each other.

An excellent example of the switching phenomenon comes from my own life. Whenever my wife and I were invited out to a friend's house for dinner, I was never ready to go by the time we had to leave. My wife always had to pressure me, saying, "Hurry up and get dressed or we'll be late!" Then, I would grudgingly go and get ready, while my wife would be mumbling, "I hate being late..." Sure enough, when we got into the car, we would only have ten minutes to get there (which was never enough time to get where we were going). On top of it I'd drive very fast to try to be on time, which further stressed out my wife. Most of the time, we ended up being late. We got the reputation from our friends as being "the late ones."

One day, my wife decided she wasn't going to be the one to motivate me to get ready anymore. She stayed in her office working until way past the time for her to be ready to leave. I suddenly felt panicked and ran into her office saying, "Hurry up or we'll be late!" She shrugged and went to get ready. Quite the reversal!

At the time, we weren't yet aware of the beliefs behind our behaviors, but one thing was certain: we both had some beliefs about being on time which ensured that we would always be late. Eventually, we discussed what we thought our beliefs were. My wife uncovered the belief that "I must always be in a rush to get somewhere." My belief was that "I have all the time in the world." These beliefs worked extremely well together since my lack of awareness that time is important when we have made plans fed my wife's need to always be under stress whenever we go out. Our limiting beliefs about being on time were reinforced by our complementary behaviors.

What was even more amazing was that when she took on the behavior of my belief ("I have all the time in the world"), I instinctively took on the behavior of her belief ("I must always be in a rush"). In essence, we reinforced our limiting beliefs about time with our respective behaviors. It didn't really matter who exhibited what behavior, as long as our beliefs were being mutually fulfilled.

Her turning the tables on me finally made me understand how she felt whenever we were late. I suddenly realized the pressure she must have felt. It also made me notice that we had a limiting belief problem that we both fed into. After that night, we started discussing ways of dealing with our beliefs about time. As a result, I gradually took more responsibility for being ready while she stopped putting pressure on me. Because we both empathized with each other's position and understood our own responsibility in our lateness problem, we were able to take steps to resolve it.

"Switching" behaviors between partners can expose limiting beliefs in our relationships.

Using the switching phenomenon helped us bring the subconscious beliefs we had about time into our conscious minds. Because we became aware of how our complementary beliefs about being on time fed each other on a subconscious level (while annoying us on a conscious level), we were able to start changing them.

EMPOWERING ATTRACTION

It's fascinating what we do when we are unaware of our limiting beliefs. We may feel that the behavior of the people around us is unacceptable and while this may be true, we are getting precisely what we subconsciously need in order to satisfy our beliefs. But there's hope! The law of attraction works as well with our empowering beliefs as it does with our limiting ones. If we have empowering relationship beliefs, we will attract people into our lives (or raise our children) in a way that will make our relationships with them thrive.

For example, if we believe that "In order to be loved I have to love myself first," we will then attract people into our lives who mirror our own belief by being respectful and centered. They know that the most effective way to show us love is by respecting and appreciating us for who we are. It is highly unlikely that they will ever do anything to hurt our self-esteem because if they did, they would be going against the very quality that attracted them to us in the first place.

Since the law of attraction works equally well in both directions, for these people to receive love from us they also have to take good care of themselves; in other words, they have to show us that they love themselves first. In the same way limiting beliefs feed on each other, empowering beliefs feed on each other as well, which creates relationships that improve over time with little effort other than to keep nurturing our empowering beliefs.

If we are in a disempowering relationship and we start reinventing ourselves by replacing our limiting beliefs with empowering ones, in many cases, this alone will influence our partners to change for the better as well. The law of attraction that originally got us together can still do its magic. If we are determined to make a positive change in our lives, then our partners may sense it and begin to make their own adjustments to adapt to our new beliefs.

However, if our partners aren't as open-minded as we are about change, their limiting beliefs may force them to undermine our efforts (which could be very demoralizing). What's important to remember in these times is that our partners have not necessarily made a conscious decision to undermine us. They are likely reacting to our change on a subconscious level and may not even be aware of what it is they are doing or why they are behaving the way they are. As we learned in the chapter entitled *Dealing with Criticism*, oftentimes, there is a period of transition when our partners might become more difficult and we have to remain persistent in our efforts.

We need to remember that we have a better chance at succeeding than our partners have at undermining us, since we have made the decision to change on a conscious level. Because our partners may not be conscious of why or what they are fighting against, they don't have as strong a foundation to stand on as we do. Eventually, they will start to adapt naturally to the new dynamics in the relationship.

THE LAW OF RESISTANCE

We should never be afraid to grow in our relationships out of the fear of changing the "status quo." If the people around us want to support us on our path of growth, then they will adapt to our empowering change. If they purposely try to discourage us, then we have to learn to accept them for who they are and, if they eventually stray away from us, we have to be prepared to let them go their own way.

The reason we have to let some people go from our lives is that they no longer complement our beliefs. Since we are changing inside, the people around us have to learn to accept and adapt to the change. If they make a conscious decision not to, then the law of attraction is working as its opposite: *The Law of Resistance*. Because we have changed, the people who were once important to us no longer feel comfortable around us. Our changing has, in a sense, seriously challenged their deeply held belief that it's impossible to change. Since they don't want to acknowledge that it is possible to change, they no longer feel attracted to us, but rather, resistant.

However, we shouldn't worry that we'll end up alone in the world. There will always be others who will support our path of growth. As we replace more and more limiting relationship beliefs with empowering ones, we will discover that people who are on a similar path to ours will naturally gravitate towards us. In life, we always seem to attract what is necessary to fulfill our beliefs (the empowering ones as well as the limiting ones). We don't have to make much of an effort for the law of attraction to work for us, and we don't have to worry that it isn't working. The law of attraction, like the law of gravity, never fails.

PART TWO REVIEW

If you have uncovered one or two limiting beliefs about your relationships as a result of reading the chapters or doing the experiments in Part 2, write them down below (we'll be using this information later on in the book):

_____

_____

_____

_____

PART 3

REINVENTING YOUR CAREER

*"The most effective form of competition is with oneself.
The aim is not to win or lose, but instead, to grow"*

CHAPTER 3.1
WHEN OPPORTUNITY KNOCKS

In the same way that we are influenced by societal and inherited beliefs in our relationships, we are also subject to these kinds of beliefs when it comes to our career. Whenever we are trying to achieve a goal, we often have to fight against disempowering beliefs that we adopted from our environment. In Part 3, we are going to look at ways to dispel many of these beliefs and we are also going to propose more empowering alternatives for pursuing and achieving our goals. Although this part of the book is entitled *Reinventing Your Career,* it's not just restricted to what we do for a living; it applies equally to all areas of achievement in our lives.

THE GO-GETTER TRAP

One time at a party my wife and I were hosting, I was chatting with a friend of ours whom I hadn't seen in months. She was trying to find the meaning of a dream that she was still mulling over from the previous night, and asked me if I wouldn't mind helping her figure it out. I told her that I would give it my best shot.

Given the puzzled look on her face, I thought she was going to tell me some kind of surreal story, but the dream turned out to be quite straightforward. It began with my friend waiting at a bus stop for Bus #24 to take her downtown for an appointment. Every few minutes a different bus approached the stop, but it was never the one she was waiting for. After a while, she started to get impatient because she thought she was going to be late for her appointment. More buses came, but again none of them were Bus #24. She became increasingly frustrated because she knew that unless her bus showed up soon, she would miss her appointment altogether. A new stream of buses arrived, but hers was nowhere to be seen. Now at the peak of her frustration, she was ready to snap. The next thing she knew she was lying in bed and realized that it had all been a dream.

Coincidentally, around the same time my wife and I were having the party, I was working on the concepts for this very chapter. As I listened to my friend, it dawned on me that her dream could be the perfect metaphor for this chapter's central idea. So I offered my own interpretation of her dream to see if it resonated for her.

I explained that when we are very goal oriented, we tend to fall into a trap I call the "Go-getter Trap." We are so intent on achieving our goals that our focus of concentration becomes very narrow; in other words, we establish a path in our minds between us and the goal we are pursuing and refuse to allow anything to steer us away from it. While this approach sounds effective in principle, a problem occurs when we become so stuck on *how* we will achieve our goals that we end up missing the opportunities that fall outside of our line of focus. These other alternatives are ones that we might not have considered yet, but that could also get us to our destination. We often overlook these other paths even though sometimes they could get us to our goal faster than our original plans.

We also tend to overlook the possibility that the path we have charted for ourselves might be incorrect. We may think it will take us to our goal, but in reality we might be going down the wrong way. Because we are closing our minds off to what is happening outside of our narrow focus, sometimes we may miss the best chances to get us where we want to go.

The metaphor I saw in my friend's dream was that Bus #24 represented the route she had chosen to take her to her appointment. On some level, she had decided that taking this bus was the *only* means by which she could reach her destination. All the other buses that she let pass by represented missed opportunities because one of those buses could have taken her there also, maybe even quicker than #24. But because these buses had never been part of her original plan, she didn't even entertain the thought of taking them instead. I suggested to my friend that perhaps she was having trouble achieving a goal in some area of her life, and she was so determined to do it in one specific way that she wasn't seeing other alternatives that were also available to her.

When I was done with my interpretation of the dream, her face was beaming. She said that she had just realized that her dream was a reflection of the problems she was experiencing lately in her career. She went on to explain that in trying to drum up new business, she had set a much higher sales quota than she had ever attempted before. Since she had been very successful achieving all her prior quotas, she decided to stick to the same techniques that had given her success in the past. What she was discovering, however, was that it was becoming increasingly difficult for her to meet her new goal. She couldn't understand why she was having so much trouble, in spite of having the same level of motivation, the same amount of focus, and the same "go-getterness" as before.

What she was beginning to realize was that she had focused so intensely on the one way she knew of achieving her sales quota that she wasn't open to other approaches that might take her to the new level more effortlessly. These other approaches might have been right under her nose all along (like the buses in her dream), but she didn't see them as opportunities because they weren't part of her original plan.

SEEING THE OPPORTUNITIES

Initially, it may be difficult for us to accept that we could miss opportunities by being too focused, since we have always been taught that the more focused we are the higher our chances for success. We think that *only* by focusing very strongly in one direction will we get the results we want. But the fact that we are open to other opportunities doesn't mean that we have to take our attention away from our goal, or that we are tampering with our chances of getting the results we want; it simply means that we are acknowledging that we could come across better ways to achieve our goal than what we have already chosen.

We can get the results we want AND be open to changing our plans.

The picture below illustrates the "Go-getter Trap." By focusing too narrowly on the goal at hand we only get to see the steep staircase right ahead of us, but we fail to notice the elevator just a few feet away that can get us to our goal faster and with less effort.

A more effective way of achieving our goals is to start with a plan for how to get us where we want to go, and then make sure that we remain open to other opportunities that come up along the way. While our tendency might be to dismiss them at first because they aren't part of our plans, it's important to remember that these other opportunities might help us get to our goals even faster than what we originally planned. *The trick is to stay determined to achieve our goals regardless of how we achieve them.*

If we spend our time beating our heads against a wall as we are trying to achieve a goal in *only* one way, we end up fighting our lives instead of enjoying them. This is why other opportunities are so important to acknowledge and consider. Incidentally, being open to other alternatives doesn't mean that we should be scattered and go in whatever direction the wind blows. It just means that we are aware that *there are* other ways to get to the same destination. We'd be surprised to find out how much we can learn by taking a different route. Sometimes, even when we think our original goal is so far off that it seems it'll never happen, if we remain open to other opportunities, we may be surprised to find it fall right down into our laps.

This reminds me of a story that a man, Rick, once told me during a business flight to the south. He had joined his company many years back along with a friend. They had both wanted to climb up the corporate ladder to reach high management positions, but as it turned out, they took two very different approaches. Rick decided that he wanted to remain in his southern town because he loved it there, and as a result, he only pursued opportunities for local promotions. His friend loved the town as much, but was open to moving elsewhere within the company if the right opportunity for promotion arose, knowing that he could always return if he didn't like it.

Within a couple of years, they both got their first promotion to management. About three years later, the company started to expand its operations, but the expansion was taking place in the west. Rick's friend realized that there were more opportunities elsewhere in the country, so he moved to a western town and was promoted to senior manager. About three years later, the company started expanding again, this time to the east. Rick's friend moved again to take a new director position out east. Meanwhile, the company branch in the south where Rick worked at hadn't changed much. He was limited to moving laterally when he wanted a new challenge because there weren't any local opportunities to move up the ladder. After another three or four years went by, the company started expanding its operations back in the south. As a result, a new vice-president position opened up in town, and Rick's friend, who was now a director in the east, applied for it and got it.

After ten years had gone by, Rick and his friend were both still working for the same company and they were both living in their southern home town. However, one of them had quadrupled his income and had become a company vice-president, whereas the other had only doubled his income and was still a manager.

Even though they both originally had the same goal and the same qualifications, their results were so radically different because they looked at their opportunities differently. While one refused to consider other ways of achieving his goal, the other was open to different possibilities. Rick didn't consider any opportunities that fell outside his original plan. He wanted to remain in his home town because he was very comfortable there and wasn't willing to consider moving out, even if it was only as a temporary measure.

His friend, on the other hand, did consider the other opportunities, even though he would have loved to stay in his home town as much as Rick. The most interesting thing about this story is that even though Rick's friend had to move three times in the course of his career, he ended up achieving his original goal much faster than Rick's and ended up in the same town where both had always wanted to live!

BEING CLEAR

Once we have a goal in mind, a plan to get us going, and decide to be open to the opportunities around us, we then have the right tools to get the results we want. But the results aren't going to happen unless we are persistent.

Many of us are excellent starters, but poor finishers. We get all gung-ho at the beginning of a project. We choose the goals, make the plans, and we get going, but as soon as we hit a snag and it starts taking longer than we expected, we lose steam. If after a while we don't get the results we expect, then we abandon our old goal and start from scratch with a fresh one. When we hit a snag with the new goal, we drop it too and go after yet another one.

The reason we allow ourselves to fall into this vicious cycle is that we aren't clear as to *why* we want to achieve our goals. If we aren't clear about why we really want something, then when we are faced with all the everyday challenges necessary to achieve it, we start losing motivation. Next thing we know, our determination starts to slip because we are not sure anymore if what we are pursuing is really worth all the effort. And finally, without our determination, we lose our drive. Once our drive is gone, our goal loses its allure and we end up giving up on it.

Even having all the skills and the resources necessary to achieve our goals won't guarantee success, if we are not clear why we really want them. For instance, ever since I was a young child, I've had a natural talent for music. Writing and playing music has always been a hobby of mine. When I got my first good paying job out of college, I slowly started buying music and sound equipment to build my own home recording studio. My goal was to record my own music and then sell it. But I wasn't really clear about why I wanted to do this, other than the fact that I knew I could do it. I knew I had the musical talent and the money required to achieve this goal.

However, many years have gone by since then and my sound recording equipment is still sitting in my office collecting dust. Even though I knew I could record my own music, I wasn't really clear about why I wanted to do this. As a result, my drive went away and I never ended up achieving this goal.

Getting results is more a function of how clear our wants are than of all the resources and skills we may have at our disposal. When our wants are clear to us, we develop empowering beliefs around them. In turn, these beliefs provide us with the conviction necessary to see us through the obstacles. And there will be obstacles. But no matter how long it takes to overcome them, if we are clear about what we want and *why* we want it, we'll never lose sight of our goals. As a result, our determination and drive will remain with us through to the very end.

THE OPPOSITE RULES!

POPULAR RULE

The more focused we are on our path, the more success-ful we will be at achieving our goals.

OPPOSITE RULE

By making our plans flexible and open to unplanned-for possibilities, we could end up achieving our goals even faster.

EXPERIMENT:
MAKING YOUR WANTS CLEAR

The goal of this experiment is to become clear about your wants so that you have the determination you need to get results. The best way of doing this is to look at the reasons why you want to achieve your goal. A strong enough reason combined with an openness to other opportunities makes achieving goals that much easier.

• Write down a goal you want to achieve in the near future:

"I want _____ "

• Write three brief reasons WHY you want this goal to happen:

1 _____

2 _____

3 _____

These are your empowering beliefs for attaining the goal. These reasons are important to keep in mind when you come up against an obstacle. It may mean the difference between giving up and carrying on.

• Opportunities: What possible things do you have in your life right now that could help you achieve your goal?

_____

_____

_____

• For those of you who are more visually oriented, here's another option: create a goal book with pictures of the things you want to have or achieve (use magazine clippings or photos). Many times seeing a picture of what you want can help you visualize the outcome in a clearer way than just keeping it in your mind.

Chapter 3.2
How Green Is the Grass
on This Side of the Fence?

For some strange reason, a lot of us have managed to adopt the habit of thinking that the grass is always greener on the other side of the fence. Whenever we achieve something in life we are proud of, we always seem to find soon after people who have achieved what we have except better, faster, and higher. Then, we convince ourselves that our achievements are never good enough.

While it's true that there will always be someone who is more experienced than we are, who makes more money, who has a higher position, and so on, the reverse is also true. There will always be someone who is less experienced, who makes less money, and who has a lower position. And yet, we somehow manage to set ourselves up so that we always end up at the short end of the stick.

Sometimes we even sell ourselves short on purpose to prevent any potential chance for disappointment. For example, an actor friend of mine was playing the lead role in a theater production that was the highlight of her career at the time. After opening night, we all went out to celebrate. The performance had been excellent and you could see the excitement in her face. However, when the time came for her to share this excitement with the group, all she did was to emphasize to everybody the fact that she could have acted better.

Why do we have this tendency to sell ourselves short and downplay our achievements? Why do we convince ourselves that our achievements are never good enough?

THE PUBLIC ENEMIES OF ACHIEVEMENT

The answer to these questions lies in three basic fears that are single-handedly responsible for curbing our potential for achievement: *our fear of criticism, our fear of losing,* and *our fear of rejection.* These fears are based on limiting beliefs that have been passed down to us from generation to generation. They have been conditioned into our minds so deeply that it may seem like they are legitimate facts of life. However, they are nothing but smoke screens that can be dissipated very easily once we become aware of how they work in our minds.

PUBLIC ENEMY #1: FEAR OF CRITICISM

Fear of criticism is the fear of being told that what we have achieved isn't good enough. This fear makes us downplay our accomplishments because we subconsciously believe that in doing so we'll be lessening the chance of getting any criticism. Oftentimes, it even stops us from attempting to achieve anything new to begin with, so that we can altogether eliminate the possibility of being criticized. In order to overcome this fear in our lives, we first have to take a look at how we perceive criticism itself.

Sometimes, no matter how much effort and time it has taken us to accomplish something, we can manage to get down on ourselves within seconds of being criticized. We allow criticism to have such an impact on our lives because we feel as if we are not measuring up to some universal standard of excellence. We feel like we have failed to hit some obscure yardstick used to measure how everybody is supposed to do. We rationalize that the criticism must be "right" or else the person who made it wouldn't have thought of it. If we were truly "good enough," then the criticism would not have crossed their minds to begin with.

The fact is that there is no universal standard for excellence. All we are contending with is somebody's opinion based on their own experience and their own judgment. Earlier, in the chapter entitled *Dealing with Criticism,* we learned that a criticism is simply a reflection of someone else's beliefs. Whether the people making the criticisms are deemed to be experts in the field or just members of our own families voicing their opinions, both are still using their own beliefs as the basis for their judgments.

A criticism reflects somebody's opinion about an event and is based <u>solely</u> on their beliefs.

As an example, I was reading the theater listings one day and I came across a new play called *The Widow Judith* which had recently opened in town. I wanted to find out more about it, so I picked up copies of the two main entertainment magazines in the city to read the reviews. What I found was rather curious. Here are the transcriptions of the critiques (incidentally, both reviews came out on the same day):

Eye Weekly *"Name of Play: The Widow Judith. Any play based on the biblical Book of Judith, in which a Hebrew Joan of Arc single-handedly routs the invading Assyrians, might be laden by some rather weighty source material. But let's get one thing straight. The Widow Judith is a comedy. Moreover, it's a very funny comedy, put together by a well-pedigreed cast and production team.*

Sally Clark's script seamlessly blends background with burlesque while maintaining a kind of backhanded reverence for the characters and the situations. Working with a simple yet versatile set and supported by evocative sound and costume design, the cast covers a lot of ground. [. . .]

In fact, the only real disappointment with The Widow Judith is the strong possibility that its short run might be up before it finds its audience. It's not unusual for a good play to die from lack of support before it's really had a chance. This is definitely a show that everyone deserves to see, and perhaps with a little luck and a few prayers, more will." *(J. Kilmartin, Feb. 12'98, Vol. 7/No. 18)*

Now Magazine *"Widow bores to death: Sally Clark's cliché-a-minute script about Judith—the beautiful, Biblical Jewish widow who saves her hometown by beheading an enemy leader—lacks subtlety, subtext and even minimal standards for acceptable writing. To say it feels like a comedy skit quickly penned by theology undergrads is being generous.*

Neither a feminist revision of a patriarchal text nor a satisfying parody, the play lacks raison d'être. A barely developed theme about

*immigration and assimilation is lost amidst unfunny jokes and
gratuitous flashes of skin.*

*Clark—who labored on this work for eight years—and director
Brian Richmond seem to be aiming for light satire with a touch of
seriousness. Too bad they didn't follow Tom Stoppard and tell the
story only through servants' eyes. Lord knows, the only fresh
performances come from that camp, with Neil Barclay as a control
queen eunuch, and Keira Loughran doubling as a girlish Susannah
and a tough-talking harem babe." (G. Sumi, Feb. 12'98, Vol. 17/No.
24)*

These are the words of two theater experts from well reputed
entertainment magazines. They both saw the same play, but the
reviews came out at opposite ends of the spectrum. Does this mean
that one reviewer is right and the other one is wrong? Hardly. Each
reviewer is simply voicing his own opinion of the play based on each
of their own experiences, interpretations, and their own perceptions
of events; in other words, *their own beliefs*.

If we let people's opinions (even when they happen to be the
experts in the field) affect how we feel about our achievements, then
we are in for quite a roller coaster ride of emotions. We get a nice
comment one moment and our self-esteem goes up; we get a negative
comment the next and it comes back down again; and the cycle
continues. That's hardly a recipe for having a fulfilling life.

The truth is, if we buy into the criticism and let it get us down, we
are only doing it because on some level we believe that the critics are
right. Their criticism matches up perfectly with a belief we already
have—what I referred to earlier in the chapter entitled *The Law of
Attraction* as "complementary beliefs." Just think, for example, that
if we always make an excellent chicken dish and believe ourselves to
be good cooks, and someone says—"This chicken tastes awful.
You're a terrible cook!"—chances are we won't believe them
because we know deep inside that we make a good chicken. We
might say to ourselves in response, "Well, I guess they just don't like
my kind of cooking" and we move on not really affected by the
comment. What this shows is that our beliefs about our ability as
cooks do not fulfill the person's criticisms. Consequently, we don't
feel bad about ourselves.

If, on the other hand, we feel insecure about our abilities in the
kitchen and don't believe we can make anything worth eating, then
we will accept the criticism because that person's beliefs fulfill our

own insecurities. As a result of being criticized, we might now say to ourselves, "Who am I kidding... I'll never be able to cook anything that tastes any good" and decide that we don't really belong in the kitchen. In this scenario, the criticism was exactly the same, but because our beliefs matched what the critic said, we ended up feeling bad about ourselves and our potential as good cooks.

A criticism can't hurt us, unless
we have a belief that fulfills it.

In essence, **no comment can hurt us *unless* a part of us believes it to be true.** It's not the fact that someone criticizes us that makes us lose confidence in our abilities, but the fact that we *believe* that he or she is right. The problem gets compounded when we aren't aware of our own beliefs because we end up trusting the critic's. Ultimately, we are letting someone else determine how we feel about our own accomplishments. Obviously, this doesn't help us achieve our goals any faster.

RELEASING CRITICISM

A good way of curbing our fear of criticism is to start assessing ourselves by our own standards instead of giving that job to others. We can do so by:

- Being aware that people's criticisms are simply a reflection of their own beliefs. They have more to do with themselves than they have to do with us.

- Being aware that if we let someone's criticism affect us, it's probably because we have a limiting belief that fulfills their opinion of us. Our negative response provides a clue that this is something we need to look at.

- Developing our own internal reference point to measure how we are doing, and developing our own personal standard of excellence that applies to no one else but ourselves (refer to the experiment at the end of the chapter entitled *Good News and Bad News* to start creating your internal reference point).

When we recognize that we can choose how we respond to criticism and that we can celebrate our achievements based on our own definition of success, we'll be able to concentrate on developing our own abilities, instead of hiding them because we fear we won't measure up to some "universal" standard outside of our control.

PUBLIC ENEMY #2: FEAR OF LOSING

Fear of losing is the fear that somebody else will get better results than we will. This fear comes into play when we are in a situation where others are pursuing the same goals as we are. When we have the fear of losing, we feel that we can only achieve success by beating our competitors. Or worse, if we don't "deem" ourselves to be competitive with the rest of the people in our field, then we may not bother trying at all.

The problem with this fear is that even when we compete with others and win, the triumph may actually be limiting our growth. When we focus on trying to beat someone else, we are not focusing on reaching our own potential. Instead, we are satisfied with just being evaluated as better than our competitors. As a result, our focus is solely based on beating others and not on our own progress. For instance, if we have the fear of losing, we will often feel better winning a poorly played tennis match where we have shown no improvement in skill, than losing an excellently played match where we have shown a dramatic improvement in our game.

A great story that clearly illustrates how this kind of competition can hinder our own potential, comes from the movie *The Right Stuff*—a highly acclaimed docudrama about the early beginnings of the American space program. When NASA began recruiting young men to become the first astronauts for the space agency, they made candidates go through an intense battery of endurance tests as part of the selection process.

In one scene in the movie, eight to ten candidates take part in a test where they have to hold their breath for the longest possible time. They are told that the current record is 91 seconds. After the first minute into the test, about half the candidates have run out of breath. As the seconds tick away, the camera shows most of the remaining candidates giving up one by one, except for a young test pilot. The camera now pans to his face as he stares at the clock in front of him. The seconds tick away as he struggles for every last gasp of air in his lungs. The hand in the clock is now showing 89 seconds, 90 seconds. His face is getting redder and redder. 91 seconds...92 seconds...93 seconds. He made it! He takes a huge breath and immediately starts congratulating himself for his feat. He has beaten everybody else and broken the previous record of 91 seconds by two full seconds!

After he regains his composure, however, he realizes that there are still two other candidates at the other end of the table holding their breath. After 120 seconds the two men are still going strong. He looks at them in total disbelief. After a few more seconds pass, a new record is then set at 128 seconds.

By focusing on beating the record, the young test pilot robbed himself out of finding out what his true potential was because he gave up as soon as he achieved his 93 second goal. This limited focus demonstrates how the fear of losing can restrict our growth. All he wanted to do was beat the record, thinking that this was enough to beat his competitors. Little did he know that just beating the record for the sake of it was no guarantee that he would have the best time. Meanwhile, there were two other candidates working at testing their true potential. In doing so, they managed to achieve their personal best.

To eliminate the fear of losing from our lives we have to stop competing against others and start competing with ourselves.

Truly successful athletes (those with staying power) don't view their opponents as the drivers of their success. Before a competition they manage to shut out the world and turn completely inward. And when they are competing, the last thing they are thinking about is their opponent. Actually, chances are they are not even "thinking" much, but are just concentrating on doing what they know how to do, but better, more freely, more naturally than the last time they did it. Interestingly, when you ask these athletes what motivates them to get great results consistently, they always say that they just love to win; they never say that they love to beat their opponents.

RELEASING THE STIGMA OF "LOSING"

A good way of letting go of the fear of losing is to stop comparing ourselves to others. We can achieve this by:

- Realizing that focusing on how others are doing can limit our ability to reach our own potential.

- Letting go of our need for external validation.

- Starting to trust our own judgment.

We can gain much more personal strength by focusing on how *we* are doing than by focusing on how others are doing. We can start curbing our fear of losing by realizing that it's much more empowering to concentrate on improving ourselves than on beating others.

PUBLIC ENEMY #3: FEAR OF REJECTION

Fear of rejection is the fear of being unwanted. This fear makes us do what we think others want us to do instead of doing what *we* want to do. Since we allow others the choice of accepting or rejecting us based on what we say or do, we end up refraining from accomplishing anything that we think might be a threat to them. A small voice speaks at the back of our minds saying, "What if we become so good at what we do that other people resent us and then reject us as a result?"

This fear makes us do what is "expected" of us, instead of doing what we really want to do. It keeps us from challenging ourselves because we can't bear the thought of others not liking us if we succeed. It can also stop us from speaking our minds if we have a different view or opinion than somebody else whom we perceive to be in a position of respect or authority. Since we are afraid we might be rejected for our different thoughts, we may not voice them; therefore, our thoughts and opinions, however valid, remain unexpressed.

THE ROOTS OF REJECTION

To understand how the fear of rejection works at undermining our desire to succeed, we have to look at why we feel hurt when we are rejected.

Ever since childhood, our achievements have been measured by how much we please others. For instance, when it came to getting good grades in school, gaining the approval of the teacher was often a higher motivator than realizing our own potential. As a result, we were only "accepted" (recognized as good students) if we met some external set of criteria. Hardly ever were we encouraged to reach our potential for our own enjoyment and desire. Since many of our teachers were raised under the same old beliefs, where living up to somebody else's expectations took precedence over living up to our own potential, they didn't really understand the concept of self-motivation. If they didn't understand how to truly motivate themselves from within, how could they possibly teach *us* this skill? We never learned how to go after something we wanted just because that was what we *wanted* to do. Instead, we learned to go after what was expected of us.

Because of this childhood conditioning, where in order to be accepted (or not be rejected) we had to fulfill somebody else's expectations, a good number of us grew into our adult lives with the fear of rejection. We fear that if we achieve something that is "outside the norm" as dictated to us by the expectations of our families, friends, loved ones, bosses, and so on, then we won't be wanted by them anymore. We deal with this fear either by blocking ourselves from attempting what we truly want and doing instead "what we are expected" to please others, or by doing what we want to do, but not allowing ourselves to become "too" successful at it.

What we have to realize is that **by pursuing our own wants, we have a much better chance of reaching our potential than if we do what's "expected" of us.** For starters, we won't be as vulnerable to rejection, since we'll be responsible to no one but ourselves for our accomplishments. Secondly, we'll feel much more motivated because we'll be doing what *we* truly want to do, rather than what *someone else* wants us to do. Finally, we'll feel better about ourselves because we'll be in control of our choices.

Keep in mind, however, that there will always be people who will reject us in our lives. The fact is that if we are following our own path and doing what we believe is right for us, some people may not like it and try to limit their contact with us. As we learned in the chapter entitled *The Law of Attraction*, when we start changing our beliefs to begin living the life we aspire to, some people around us may react adversely because they are not used to us being true to ourselves and going for what we want. However, once we can accept that what others think is immaterial to how well we are doing in our lives, then we'll be no longer be discouraged by the rejection that may sometimes come our way.

LEAVING REJECTION BEHIND

Wouldn't it be wonderful if we could leave our fear of rejection behind? We wouldn't feel so afraid of being isolated by others as we pursue our deepest wants. We can achieve this by:

- Starting to believe in our own uniqueness, knowing we all have different dreams and paths to our goals.

- Giving ourselves permission to do what we want to do and not what's expected of us, knowing that we are fully capable of choosing the direction for our lives.

- Knowing that people's rejections reveal beliefs about themselves and not about us.

By building trust in our own uniqueness and not worrying about whether the people in our lives approve of the choices we make or not, we will develop the self-confidence necessary to become immune to rejection.

We can eliminate the fears of criticism, losing, and rejection from our lives by learning to focus on ourselves and by letting go of the need for external validation and direction. Once we start taking our own cues from what *we* want to achieve, we'll feel happier and more fulfilled in our lives because we'll know we are doing what's best for us and no longer feel as if the grass is greener elsewhere.

THE OPPOSITE RULES!

POPULAR RULE		**OPPOSITE RULE**
It always hurts to be criticized.	➡	Criticisms can't hurt us, unless we have beliefs that fulfill them.
Competing against others is a powerful motivator for reaching our goals.	➡	Competing with ourselves is an even more powerful motivator.
A rejection is an indication that we are not good enough.	➡	A rejection simply reveals that our beliefs are not compatible with someone else's.

EXPERIMENT:
YOUR PERSONAL FEARS

The goal of this experiment is to look at those personal fears that are stopping you from pursuing and achieving your goals. We have explored the common fears of criticism, losing and rejection and here is an opportunity for you to look at how specifically they function in your life.

- Name your most important goal:

  _____

- List all the reasons why this goal can't happen and alongside it write CR, LOS, or REJ depending on whether the reason you believe it can't happen reflects the fear of criticism, losing or rejection:

  _____   _____

  _____   _____

  _____   _____

  _____   _____

  _____   _____

  _____   _____

- You might find that one category is more prominent than the others in your reasons why you believe you can't achieve your goal. Write your most "popular" category:

  _____

- With this knowledge, what do you think your primary limiting belief is?

  _____

  _____

CHAPTER 3.3
FIXING OUR PROCRASTINATION PROBLEM

Painfully familiar to so many of us, procrastination is a problem that never seems to go away. Simply defined, it is the habit of putting off taking the necessary actions to achieve a given result. Also known as the "silent killer" of achievement, procrastination works by quietly undermining its key pillars—our determination and drive. Although sometimes it may seem to be a difficult habit to control, we can learn to manage procrastination very effectively and eventually we can even remove it altogether from our lives.

Before we can begin this process, however, we need to explore how this habit is intimately linked to one of the biggest fears in human nature: *the fear of success*.

PROCRASTINATION AND THE FEAR OF SUCCESS

Why would we willingly put off taking the necessary actions that would bring us closer to our goals? It just doesn't make sense to go through a huge struggle every day to motivate ourselves to do something that *we know* will benefit us. Looking a little deeper, though, we'll find that we procrastinate because we have limiting beliefs tied to our desire for achievement. In other words, on some level, *we fear succeeding*. Procrastination is quite simply the mechanism by which our fear of success manifests itself in our daily routine—the more we put off taking action towards our goals, the less we have to worry about how success will affect our lives.

Procrastination is the enforcing mechanism of our fear of success.

The fear of success is primarily based on the belief that "If we succeed, then bad things will happen to us." Behind this fear lurk many limiting beliefs about what achieving our goals will mean to us. Perhaps we believe that if we become successful, then we'll be so busy that we'll never get to see our family, or our friends will shun us because we won't be able to complain with them about money anymore, or we'll end up with some kind of health problem. Whatever our beliefs may be they cause us to develop a fear of becoming successful, and as a result we end up delaying the achievement of our goals—in other words, we procrastinate.

One day I was chatting with a very dear friend of mine who was having trouble at work dealing with procrastination. He had a good job, but was finding it very difficult to motivate himself to take his career to the next level. He wanted to move ahead in his company, but whenever an opportunity for advancement would come up, he'd put off updating his resume and always managed to miss the deadline. When I asked him why he thought he was putting things off, he confided that deep inside he was afraid of becoming too successful.

So I asked him what he meant by "becoming too successful." He went on to tell me that he was raised in a household where his father was very successful in business. However, he was also very demanding and believed that since he provided generously for his family, in return they had to comply with his every whim. As a result, he frequently alienated everybody with his hard-to-meet requests, which created a constant state of stress and anxiety at home.

Since my friend had associated success with his father's behavior, he feared that if he became successful in his own right, he would then start behaving like his father and make everybody run away from him. As a matter of fact, he feared this so much *that he was effectively stopping himself from going after anything that had any chance of making him successful.* His procrastination habit simply served the purpose of ensuring that he would never succeed.

This is just one example of the many limiting beliefs about success that we might have developed or inherited throughout our lives. Unfortunately, as if it wasn't enough having to contend with these personal fears about success, we also have to deal with the constant pressure from society to be successful. Our cultural beliefs enforce the myth that a person's worth is determined by the level of success he or she attains in life. Society cements this conditioning by celebrating with great fanfare those who have "reached" success, along with their visible rewards. Stories abound about the financial abundance, the luxury possessions, the affluent lifestyles, and the fame of many successful people. As a result, we find ourselves deadlocked between our own fears and the expectations about success that society imposes on us. Clearly, we need to find a way out of this deadlock if we are to dismantle the foundation of fear that leads to our habit of procrastination.

A NEW APPROACH TO SUCCESS

In order to stop procrastination from sabotaging our ability to succeed in life, we have to significantly change our views and beliefs about success. Specifically, **we need to stop looking at success as a goal and start looking at it as a means to a goal.** This new approach may seem a bit strange at first, since we've been conditioned for so long to view success as just an outcome. However, making success an everyday state of mind can go a long way toward easing our fears about it. Let's illustrate with an example how this new way of looking at success can work for us. Let's say that we've been in our present job for a long time and now want a change, so we embark on the search for a new job. If we make success the goal of our search (that is, we believe that we will achieve success only if we land a new job), then we may find ourselves procrastinating when it's time to make or update our resume, look for job ads, find information about potential employers, read that popular book on interviews, and so on. Even if we force ourselves to do all these things (because we really hate the job we are doing right now), it's highly unlikely that we will present ourselves to potential employers as the image of success they want to see. Instead, we'll probably convey a sense of neediness and apprehension.

If, by contrast, we choose to adopt the empowering belief that success is the *means* to our goal, not just the goal itself, then we will approach our job search with a "successful mindset." For instance, we'll look at a new job as a means for advancement, not as a last-ditch effort to get out of a job we hate. Also, with this new mindset, we may actually start getting other offers from our place of work or even calls from headhunters to whom we've been referred. And when we do finally go for the job interview, we'll already be conveying an image of success because we won't "need" the new job to make us successful—we will already <u>feel</u> successful. Our behavior and attitude will reflect the belief that the job we are looking for is already ours. Instead of allowing the achievement of success be the builder of our self-worth, we'll make our self-worth become the *reflection* of an already successful mindset.

Once we embrace success as a state of mind instead of an outcome, our fear of success will not fulfill any purpose any more and it will quietly begin to fade away. As a result, procrastination will cease to be a problem for us. Should it ever come back, we can use it as a sign that we are slipping back into the old way of thinking and take the opportunity to reinforce our new success mindset.

Procrastination's Close Cousin

Another condition that undermines our ability for achievement by also forcing us into a state of inaction, is the emotion of *being over-whelmed*. This emotion can be described as the sense of anxiety that we feel when there are many more things to accomplish than we can possibly handle.

Like procrastination, becoming overwhelmed is also the result of limiting beliefs. However, this time our beliefs aren't tied to the fear of success, but to its flip side—*the fear of failure*. This fear is the constant worry that unless we achieve absolutely everything that we have set out to do, we will be deemed a failure. Since society perceives failure as an outcome to be avoided at all cost, we feel that we have to become supermom, superdad, superemployee, and so on, as a form of insurance against it. We think that by doing everything perfectly all the time, nobody will ever have the grounds to label us a failure. As a result, we feel so overwhelmed by all the things that we need to take care of, that we end up paralyzed with anxiety.

---

*The emotion of being overwhelmed
is a reflection of our fear of failure.*

Clearly, this emotion does not help us achieve our goals any more than procrastination does, but luckily it can be diffused very effectively. How do we go about it? As it is the case with success, we need to look at failure from an entirely new perspective.

A NEW APPROACH TO FAILURE

The reason that we label failure as "bad" and "unwanted" is that we've been conditioned over many years with these negative labels. As we recall from the chapter entitled *Good News and Bad News,* events aren't "good" or "bad" in and of themselves. They are simply what we perceive them to be according to our own beliefs. In essence, failure is neither bad nor good, but just what *we* make it to be.

Sometimes what we perceive to be a failure may be a step in the right direction ("a blessing in disguise"), even if we can't see the opportunity in it at the time. We may label a certain outcome to be a failure because it's not in the direction we had anticipated, but, as we learned earlier in the chapter entitled *When Opportunity Knocks,* this apparent "failure" might actually be a step towards our goal. Perhaps what we learn from this failure could get us where we want to go even faster than our original plans.

Sometimes an apparent "failure" might really be a step in the right direction.

If we adopt the belief that failure can be an empowering experience, then our fear of failure will slowly start to fade away. Since we'll begin to look at our perceived "setbacks" as a chance to explore other alternatives that we might not have yet considered, we won't be so fearful about failing anymore. As a result of our new approach, those times when we feel overwhelmed will begin to decrease in number and intensity. Since we'll no longer be so concerned that we could be labeled a failure for our attempts, we'll more than likely do the best we can given our circumstances rather than feel paralyzed by the number of things we need to do.

For instance, if we have a long list of things to achieve and discover as the day progresses that we don't have enough time to do all of them, we won't feel like a failure if we don't finish absolutely everything on the list. Instead, we'll do our best to finish what we can and be open to learning any hidden lessons from the experience. Perhaps we'll realize that we shouldn't try to squeeze so much work into such a short amount of time. This may be our lesson for the future.

One of the unexpected benefits from seeing failure from an empowering perspective, is that we'll discover that we are achieving <u>more</u> things than we could ever before. Instead of feeling overwhelmed all the time, we will feel energized. Because we spend so much effort sustaining the state of anxiety associated with being overwhelmed, we never have enough energy left to do the things that actually need to be done. But once we rid ourselves from this debilitating emotion, we will have all of our energy intact to tackle the tasks at hand; and therefore we'll be able to get more things done.

STRATEGY FOR WHEN WE FEEL OVERWHELMED

As we begin to be a little easier on ourselves and gradually let go of our fear of failure, we'll find that we are going to feel overwhelmed less and less. But when the times get tough, it helps to have a little strategy to help us get back on track:

- Whenever you start feeling overwhelmed, make a do-list with those things you want to accomplish so that you have a *clear* picture of what needs to be done (as opposed to keeping things "floating" in your mind).

- Prioritize the items on your list in order of preference or importance.

- Tackle one item on the list at a time and try <u>not</u> to think about any of the others as you're doing it.

- Focus on *enjoying* the task at hand as much as you can, not on "getting it out of the way."

- Once you're done with an item on the list, check it off, and then move on to the next one using the same process.

In summary, the action of putting things off and the emotion of being overwhelmed by what needs to be done are really disguises for our fears of success and failure. Once we are able to view success as a mindset and failure as a learning opportunity, we'll begin to discover that we are procrastinating and becoming overwhelmed less and less in our daily experience.

THE OPPOSITE RULES!

POPULAR RULE		OPPOSITE RULE
Success is a state that we can only attain when we achieve something significant.	➡	Success is a mindset available to us all of the time.
Failure is something to be avoided at all cost.	➡	Failure is neither negative nor positive. Sometimes what we perceive to be a failure may be a step in the right direction.

EXPERIMENT:
CONFRONTING THE FEAR OF SUCCESS

The goal of this experiment is to face our fear of success so that we can look at the root of our procrastination. Acknowledging what we fear will happen if we achieve our goal is the first step towards releasing the need to procrastinate from our lives.

- Name a goal: _____

- List three possible scenarios that you fear will happen if you achieve your goal:

    1 _____

    2 _____

    3 _____

    These are the reasons you procrastinate. They are also clues to the limiting belief(s) you have about success.

- Using the above scenarios, try to uncover the primary limiting belief behind your fear of success and write it below:

    _____

- Example:

    Goal: I want to make $100,000 a year within 2 years.

    Three scenarios: 1. My family won't like me anymore; 2. I won't have time for fun; 3. I might become mean and demanding.

    Limiting belief: If I'm successful, I'm going to become someone I don't want to be.

- Think about an empowering belief with which you would like to replace this limiting belief and write it below:

    _____

    _____

CHAPTER 3.4
SETTING GOALS INSTEAD OF EXPECTATIONS

We all have personal aspirations. We want to have a good job with a good income, to have a comfortable lifestyle, and to be free of debt. We want the best for ourselves, our kids, and our families, and we always try to find the best means that are available to us to achieve it. Ultimately, what we all really want is to live happy and fulfilling lives and—why not—have fun in the process too.

Our troubles begin when we use expectations as a motivator for achieving what we want in life, and the results we get don't pan out exactly the way we thought they would. Since we "expect" things to go a certain way, we leave ourselves open to being hurt if they go in a different direction. In this chapter, we'll look at why setting expectations is not as effective a motivator as we think it is and we'll present a much more powerful alternative.

THE MOTIVATION PROBLEM

We seem to make expectations a central part of our lives. Whether we enter the work force, start our own business, or embark on a new hobby, we immediately begin having expectations about how far we'll get, how fast we'll get there, how much money we'll make, and so on. We think that our expectations will give us the incentive to take the necessary actions for achieving our goals. At the same time, we fear that if we *don't* set them, we won't try hard enough.

On the surface, setting expectations may appear to be a good motivator for achievement. However, it oftentimes creates the opposite effect of what was intended; that is, our expectations become a source of disappointment. By nature, expectations are very rigid. They tend to be highly polarized—we either meet them or we don't. Our expectations don't allow us to accept anything less than shining success. If we don't meet an expectation that we have set for ourselves, chances are we'll feel disappointed and likely get down on ourselves as the punishment for our failure.

Expectations are usually *very difficult to meet* and *very painful when we fail to meet them*. Whenever we set expectations, we subconsciously tie our self-esteem to getting the results we want to achieve. If we somehow manage with great effort to meet our expectations, then our self-esteem goes up a notch. But if we fail to meet them, our self-esteem takes a nose dive.

Interestingly, there seems to be a strong resemblance between "expecting" something to happen and "needing" it to happen (as we learned earlier in the chapter entitled *The Manipulationship*, "needing" something is similarly tied to our self-esteem). The following chart does a comparison between these two words:

EXPECTING	NEEDING
When we expect something, we tend to get emotionally attached to the outcome.	When we need something, we tend to get emotionally attached to the object of our need.
When we have an expectation and fail to meet it, we get down on ourselves.	When we need something and don't get it, we feel bad about ourselves.
Whenever we have an expectation, we feel that if we can't meet it, then something will be missing from our lives.	When we need something, we feel that if we can't get it then something will be missing from our lives.

As we can see from the chart on the previous page, "expecting" and "needing" are practically synonymous. When we are expecting something, we are in need of it too. As we learned earlier in *The Manipulationship*, a *need* reflects the desire to fill a void in our lives. If we are unable to fill this void, then we don't feel complete. **No wonder we feel let down when we fail to meet our expectations!** Ultimately, this is a very ineffective way of motivating ourselves to get results in our lives.

THE ADVANTAGE OF SETTING GOALS

We also learned in *The Manipulationship* that the best way to get results without tying our self-esteem to getting them is to turn our *needs* into *wants*. When we *want* something, we simply have the desire to add more to what we've already got; we are not trying to fill a void in our lives. As a result, we don't feel incomplete when we don't immediately get it. So, how can we get the results we want without setting expectations? By setting goals instead. In the same way that expectations are synonymous with "needs," goals are synonymous with "wants." Turning our expectations into goals is equivalent to turning our needs into wants.

Our goals reflect our desire to <u>add</u> something new to what we already have. Our expectations reflect our <u>need</u> to get something we are missing.

When we set goals instead of expectations, we are still going after the same results, but we are not attaching our emotions to getting them. If we don't get what we want *when* we want it, we will not perceive this as a personal failure since we are not actually "losing" anything. All we are doing is *temporarily delaying* having something to a later time. By setting goals instead of expectations, we are implicitly acknowledging that there's nothing missing in our lives. Because we are not trying to fill a void, we feel strong enough to continue pursuing our goal for as long as it takes. We are still going for what we want, mind you, but this time from a foundation of strength instead of one of neediness.

Let's use an example to illustrate the difference between setting a goal and setting an expectation. If I wish to be promoted at work to the level of manager, I could phrase my desire as either a *goal* or an *expectation*. Let's see how each choice affects my behavior:

GOAL

"I plan to be promoted to manager by the end of the year"

The goal expresses my *want* to be promoted. It places the onus for achievement on myself because it makes me focus on what *I* have to do to achieve this goal (more specifically by coming up with a plan of action). Essentially, I want to be promoted to manager by the end of the year and I will do the best I can to achieve this goal by following through on my plan.

Since now my emotions are not tied to achieving the result I want, I know that even if I don't become a manager by the end of the year, this won't constitute failure for me. All I have to do is revisit my existing plan of action to see if there are any changes I can do in the following year to make attaining my goal more certain. Perhaps I need to prove that my interpersonal skills are at the manager level, or that I can handle more than one project at a time. What's important is that I am acknowledging that there are things I can do to make it easier to achieve my goal. But, in the meantime, I feel motivated to do my present job because I don't feel anything is really missing from my life. I definitely *want* to get the promotion, but I don't *need* it as a condition for my fulfillment.

EXPECTATION

"I expect to be promoted to manager by the end of the year"

The expectation, on the other hand, expresses my *need* to get the promotion. It places the onus for achievement on somebody else. "I expect to be promoted" implies that somebody else **must give me** a promotion so that my expectation can be fulfilled. Since I feel as if someone owes me the promotion, I don't feel the desire to create a specific plan of action. I am assuming that the good work I put in every day will clinch it for me. However, as we learned earlier in the chapter entitled *The Art of Peace,* when we feel we owe someone our relationship with that person suffers. The same is true in a work relationship. If I believe my boss owes me a promotion, then he or she will feel manipulated and therefore, will be less inclined to give it. If I believe that someone owes me a promotion, then I'm not taking responsibility for my own advancement, but I'm expecting someone else to take care of it for me.

> *Setting expectations places the onus for our achievement on others, while setting goals places it on ourselves.*

Not only does having the expectation of being promoted make me not take responsibility, but it also sets me up for disappointment. If I don't become a manager by the end of the year, then I'll believe I will have failed. This sense of failure will not likely inspire me to keep trying because I'll feel that something has been taken away from me. I'll feel hurt and demotivated to do my present job. In other words, because I was emotionally attached to getting promoted, my self-esteem took a hit when I didn't get it.

Clearly, it is much more effective for us to set goals instead of expectations in our careers (and our lives), since setting goals places the responsibility for their fulfillment squarely on our shoulders. In turn, this approach allows us the freedom to go after our wants without having our self-esteem dependent on the outcome. If our expectations ever try to sneak their way back into our lives, we can acknowledge their presence and perhaps try to look at why we feel we have a void in that particular area of our lives. Once we acknowledge an expectation and then convert it into a goal, we'll discover that our emotions are no longer hostage to circumstances outside of our control.

A SUCCESS STORY

A friend of mine once related to me the following predicament he found himself in. He told me that lately he hadn't been getting the recognition at work that he used to get whenever he completed a project. His work had always been highly regarded in the past and he had come to expect this recognition to naturally come his way. As a result, he was feeling very demotivated to do his job. He feared that he would never be able to regain the level of motivation he used to enjoy earlier in his career.

In response to his concern, I asked him to look at his situation and see if he could find the *need* behind his expectation for recognition.

After thinking about it for a while, he realized that he *needed* the recognition he was looking for in order to confirm that he was still competent and skilled and to prove to himself that he that wasn't stagnating in his job.

Once he was able to uncover the need behind his expectation, I asked him to try rephrasing it as a want. He came up with: *I don't want to stagnate in my job.* I suggested that he change the want into a positive statement in order to make it more empowering. He rephrased it to: *I want to be innovative in my job.* I now asked him to begin looking for a goal that would fulfill his new want. In searching for it, he became very pensive for a few seconds, and then recounted to me that when he had joined his company, he used to be very innovative and eager, but as the years went by, he had slowly become complacent. He now realized that lately he had been feeling insecure about his competence and needed the constant recognition from his peers to alleviate this insecurity. As a result of his newfound understanding, he decided to come up with the following goal for himself: *I plan to take up projects that capitalize on my skills and that are rewarding in themselves.*

Weeks later he told me that having this goal in mind instead of the old expectation had totally changed his outlook at work. He was beginning to enjoy his job again and to depend less on having the approval of others as his motivation for achievement. He was now focusing on what *he* could do to make his time at work more fulfilling.

For him, turning his expectation into a goal was like jump-starting his career. And interestingly, even though his goal made no mention about getting recognition, he began getting more positive comments about his work than he ever did with his old expectation.

Once we start rephrasing our expectations as goals and let go of *needing* things to go a certain way, we'll be more likely to get the results we want because we are now going to go after them from a position of strength. In essence, we will free ourselves to pursue our goals without any restrictions and without negatively impacting our self-esteem.

THE OPPOSITE RULES!

POPULAR RULE

Setting expectations is a good motivator for getting results.

OPPOSITE RULE

Setting goals is a much better motivator because it doesn't hold our self-esteem hostage to getting the results.

EXPERIMENT:
SETTING GOALS

The object of this experiment is to learn how to set goals as well as to become aware of any expectations that we might have about achieving them. Setting goals begins with having a want, but also includes a plan of action.

- Write down a goal you want to achieve and a time frame:

  "I plan to _____ "

- Expectation Test:

  Ask yourself, "Will I be upset if I don't achieve this goal?"

  If you think you'll be upset (not just a bit disappointed), then write down the reason below:

  "I'll be upset because _____

  _____ "

The above statement is a clue to a limiting belief that you have about achieving your goal. This limiting belief is turning your goal into an expectation. For now, it's enough to acknowledge that you have emotions tied the achievement of your goal.

- Plan: List three things you can do to achieve your goal:

  1 _____

  2 _____

  3 _____

Do you feel any resistance to any of the steps in your plan? If you do, here's another clue to a limiting belief. What do you think this belief is?

_____

You will have an opportunity to unlearn this limiting belief later on in the book. For now, just be aware that it exists.

Chapter 3.5
Using Our Strengths to Overcome Our Weaknesses

When it comes to our jobs, no matter what we do for a living we all have strengths and weaknesses. Our strengths are those areas in which our level of confidence is high, and conversely our weaknesses are those areas in which it is low. Note that I am referring to "level of confidence" and <u>not</u> "level of skill." The reason I am stressing this point is that there is a marked tendency in society to associate a *strength* solely with the possession of skills (e.g. having people skills is a strength), and to associate a *weakness* with the lack of skills (e.g. having no time management skills is a weakness). But, if skills were the only basis behind our strengths, then every resume with the right skills would automatically land people a job without the need for conducting an interview. However, the reality in our careers is that it is primarily the *confidence* we have in ourselves that gives us the necessary drive to successfully clinch the new job, get the promotion, or achieve the higher sales volume. Our skill level comes second.

Which brings us to the subject of this chapter. Since we tend to associate *weakness* with "lack of skill" instead of "lack of confidence," whenever we take steps to overcome a weakness of ours, our first impulse is to try to "learn" the apparently missing skills. The drawback with this approach is that we are trying to fix a *skills* problem, when in reality what we have is a *confidence* problem.

We need to find a more effective approach for overcoming our weaknesses. An approach that deals with their underlying causes instead of just dealing with their symptoms.

THE LEARNING TRAP

Whenever we want to overcome some weakness of ours in order to increase our chances of getting the promotion we want, or landing the better job, or achieving the higher sales volume, we often think that all we need to do is learn a technique or skill that we "must" be missing. We assume that the reason we haven't reached the higher level yet is that we don't have sufficient knowledge in that area or that our skills aren't strong enough. Perhaps somebody has told us that learning a specific technique is exactly what we need to get us there. Unfortunately, it doesn't always work that way. While taking a class may be effective in teaching us something we don't know, like how to use a new spreadsheet program, it's not effective in helping us with something we already know about, but have low confidence in.

When we use the classic "sign up for a course" approach to conquer our weaknesses, we end up placing the onus for their resolution on something or someone else. For example, we may sign up for a course in listening skills and learn new techniques for how to listen effectively; however, when the class is over and we return to our job with all of its time pressures and interruptions, we may discover that we soon slip back to where we were before (with all the course materials neatly stored away in the "Never to be looked at again" filing drawer). Our weakness, though, is still around with us.

When we resort to external help, we fall into the trap of using the new skills as a crutch. In other words, we bestow the responsibility for overcoming our problems on something or someone else. As a result two things happen: first, we usually end up treating the visible symptoms and not the real cause of our problems; and second, by not taking responsibility for our own solution, we don't end up committing ourselves to the change. If the change doesn't last, we can always blame the teacher or the technique we learned for being ineffective. So we move on with our lives (with our weaknesses still in tow) and later on find ourselves trying some new technique only to have the same disappointing results.

In order to conquer our weaknesses permanently, we have to *take responsibility* for overcoming them. Let's begin this process by taking a closer look at the role our beliefs play behind our strengths and weaknesses.

Behind every strength of ours, there are one or more empowering beliefs that give it its power. In most cases, these beliefs were conditioned into us during our upbringing. For instance, if our parents told us repeatedly that "we can do anything we set our minds to," then this empowering belief alone will give us the strength required to achieve anything we choose to do with confidence, without necessarily having the supposedly required "prior experience."

My brother-in-law Dave is a good example of somebody with such a belief. Ever since he was a young child, he's been fascinated by computers. When he was a freshman in college, he decided to start a small computer multimedia company to make some money on the side to help pay for tuition. In this way, he wouldn't have to keep finding summer jobs. Since the Internet was just beginning to become very popular and Web site design was in high demand, he decided to offer his services as a Web site designer.

He didn't have any prior experience running a company and up until then the only Web site he had built was for his newly formed company using a friend's computer. Actually, at this point he didn't even have the required software himself. But what he did have was the strength of his belief that "he could do it" and this strength gave him the confidence necessary to get started.

After a few months had gone by, he had made a business contact through a friend that led to his first Web site contract. This was a large job that required forty different Web pages and had a tight deadline. However, his trust in his own abilities was so strong that he didn't get intimidated by the scope of the job. At that point, he bought the required software, taught himself how to use it, even hired his own dad and a friend as salaried assistants, and worked very hard off his own bedroom desk to deliver a great product for his client. Incidentally, this client has since become a repeat customer.

Our strengths reflect our empowering beliefs.

In the same way that our strengths are supported by empowering beliefs, every weakness of ours is supported by one or more limiting beliefs which undermine our confidence in ourselves. Although in some cases these beliefs are based on past experiences of failure in our lives, oftentimes they were conditioned into us during our upbringing.

For example, when Matt was in high school, his parents repeatedly pressured him to get good marks in math under the pretext that "Unless you have good marks in math, you'll never be able to get a good job." As a result of this pressure, every time he had a bad math score he felt like a total failure, partly because he had disappointed his parents and partly because he believed that now he would never be able to find a good job. Throughout Matt's working life, whenever he'd go for a job he really wanted (a "good" job), his lack of confidence would automatically kick in and undermine his chances of getting it. As a result, he'd have to settle for jobs he didn't enjoy as much. The bitter irony is that he failed to get the "good" jobs whether they required math skills or not!

Our weaknesses are primarily the reflection of our limiting beliefs, not of our lack of skills.

Since our level of confidence is ultimately a reflection of our own beliefs, we need to find an approach for overcoming our weaknesses that takes advantage of this important fact, and that allows *us* to be in charge of the process.

USING OUR STRENGTHS TO OVERCOME OUR WEAKNESSES

The most effective way to overcome our weaknesses is by using our own built-in tools to do the job. Since our weaknesses are based on limiting beliefs in certain areas of our lives, we can use the confidence we have developed from our empowering beliefs in other areas of our lives in order to help us gain strength in the areas where our level of confidence is weak. In this way, we are taking advantage of our existing strengths to "wear down" the limiting beliefs behind our weaknesses.

A few years ago, a coworker friend of mine shared a problem he was having in the office. Ron worked in the engineering department of a large corporation. At work, he was best known for his astounding power of concentration. When he was given a goal to accomplish, he would concentrate on it so fully that he would consistently get it done in record time and with excellent results.

However, he was usually criticized for his lack of customer care. If somebody called him asking for some information when he was in the middle of something, he would let his voice mail take the call and only return it several days later, whenever his schedule allowed it. Since complaints about Ron's poor response time had been mounting, his manager called him into the office to discuss the situation. As a result of this discussion, he recognized that customer care was a weakness of his and agreed to sign up for a course with the company's training department on building customer relationships.

After taking the course, he returned to his daily routine and tried as hard as possible to put the newly learned techniques into practice. However, after about two or three weeks, he started feeling annoyed again whenever somebody called and interrupted his concentration. He soon began letting his voice mail pick up the calls like in the old days. Not surprisingly, within a couple of months, the customer complaints started to build up once again.

One day Ron approached me to ask what I thought he could do to alleviate this situation at the office. I suggested that he try to find a way to use his power of concentration (his strength) in order to overcome his poor customer care (his weakness). He was intrigued by the concept and wanted to know more about it. I told him that since his strength was his great ability to concentrate on a project like no one else and achieve excellent results, he could use this strength to overcome his weakness by turning it into a "project" that he could easily handle. Ron was very excited by the sound of it and decided to give it a try. Basically, he approached the challenge following the same plan of action he would use with any other project: he clearly identified the results he wanted to achieve and gave himself a deadline in which to achieve them. So he chose a "project deadline" of three weeks starting from our meeting in order to achieve the "result" of zero customer complaints. As far as goals go, this one was really no different that any other goal he had previously tackled.

Within two weeks, he told me that all the complaints about his poor customer response had stopped. He said that many of his customers could not believe the change! From then on he went back to his regular goals, but this time around he made sure he always made room in his working day for answering or returning phone calls. It seems that in those two weeks he had developed close relationships with his customers for the first time and he didn't want to let them down by not returning their calls promptly.

In essence, Ron managed to overcome his weakness by taking advantage of his strengths, and since he did so using his very own abilities, the change was more effective and lasting.

When we use our strengths to overcome our weaknesses, we are taking responsibility for the changes we want to make, while being confident in our abilities. This is a powerful technique because it forces our minds to stop dwelling on the weakness and instead start focusing on the strength.

Can our strengths overcome our weaknesses all the time? It depends on how creative we get. The trick is to manage to turn our weakness into the object of our strength, like my friend Ron did in the above example. To get you started in this process, the experiment at the end of this chapter helps you to identify some of your strengths and weaknesses so that you can begin taking advantage of this powerful approach in your own life. Have fun with it!

THE OPPOSITE RULES!

POPULAR RULE

Learning new skills is the best way to overcome our weaknesses.

OPPOSITE RULE

Using the confidence in our strengths is an even better way.

EXPERIMENT:
STRENGTHS AND WEAKNESSES

The goal of this experiment is to start thinking about how we can use our strengths to overcome our weaknesses.

- Make a list of four things you know you have as strengths:

  1 _____ 2 _____

  3 _____ 4 _____

- Write two weaknesses you wish you didn't have:

  1 _____ 2 _____

- What do you think the limiting beliefs are behind the weaknesses?

  1 _____

  2 _____

- How can you use a strength or two to overcome a weakness?

  _____

  _____

  _____

- Example:

  Strength: I am highly organized.

  Weakness: I "freeze" when I give presentations.

  Limiting belief: What others think is more important than what I have to say.

  Using the strength to overcome the weakness: One way of using your strengths in organization in order to overcome your fear of public speaking is to prepare your presentation with your best attention to detail. By having all the information properly researched, rehearsed, and laid out in your mind, you won't have much room for self-doubt when you are standing in front of your peers. Since you will be highly confident in your knowledge, you will be focusing on the information you are presenting instead of thinking about the people in the audience.

CHAPTER 3.6

HOW TO WIN THE GAME
WITHOUT EVEN KNOWING THE RULES

Of all the human attributes available to help us strive towards our goals, confidence has the remarkable power to both pave our road to success and speed up the journey. Other attributes, such as talent, knowledge, skill, or experience, play an important role in our achievements, but they don't always have to be present for us to be successful. Confidence, however, is a consistent pattern in all successful people.

You can always find people who have achieved success without having a great deal of skill, or without having all the required knowledge, or even without having a lot of talent. But you'll never find successful people without a high degree of confidence in themselves. These people believe that their strengths outshine their weaknesses.

Conversely, there are a lot of people with great talent, knowledge, and skill who either fail repeatedly to achieve their goals or don't even make an attempt because they don't have confidence in themselves. There is an interesting quote attributed to Calvin Coolidge, the thirtieth president of the United States, that reads: "Nothing is more common than unsuccessful men with talent." The truth is that many people tend to focus so much on their weaknesses that they fail to develop enough trust in their strengths to succeed. Luckily, there is a good remedy for this condition.

Confidence is the key to developing the "success" mindset required to go for and achieve what we want, in spite of any obstacles along the way. It is like a mental steamroller that clears the path between us and our goals. Instead of stopping to beat ourselves up every time we hit a roadblock, we use the time to figure out a way around it. When we have confidence, we don't polarize our achievements as successes or failures. In fact, we see success and failure as two sides of the same coin—success becomes an indication that we have already achieved our goal, while failure becomes an indication that we are still working at it.

THE EXPERIENCE TRAP

If confidence is such an important key for achievement, then why do so many of us have trouble getting the confidence necessary to achieve our goals and dreams? The main culprit is the common societal belief which claims that "the only way we can develop confidence is through experience." This belief is based on the observation that the more experience we gain in a given area of our lives, the more confident we seem to become in it.

While the above belief sounds reasonable in principle, this approach to confidence is very limiting because it implies that we can only be confident *after* we have reached a certain level of experience. As a result, we fall into what I call *The Experience Trap:* we live our lives making experience a prerequisite for self-confidence, which causes us to "postpone" feeling confident until we have attained a given level of experience. Unfortunately, if it takes us many years to reach this level, we then end up robbing ourselves of years of feeling confident. The big irony is that this confidence would probably have gotten us much further ahead in life had we not delayed it.

To make things worse, if we also happen to be perfectionists then the experience trap becomes a vicious cycle. We postpone feeling confident until we attain the desired level of experience, only to realize once we get there that there are even higher levels we can reach. So we endlessly postpone feeling confident until we achieve that elusive "perfect" level of experience. What ends up happening is that no matter how hard we work and no matter what level of experience we attain, we *never* allow ourselves to feel confident.

How much experience do we actually need to acquire before we can feel truly confident? The answer is **none.** The only reason we make "getting experience" a prerequisite for developing confidence is that we *believe* it has to be this way. The fact is that confidence is not the result of experience. If it was, then as a rule people with more experience would have more confidence than people with less experience. However, there are too many exceptions to support this rule. For example, how can we explain the level of confidence Anna Paquin had when she portrayed the daughter of a mute woman in the movie *The Piano?* Her performance was so outstanding that she won an Academy Award at the tender age of eleven (she actually shot the movie when she was only nine years old!). If confidence were a skill to be acquired with experience, then certainly Anna Paquin could not have attained the confidence necessary to play such an important role at such a young age, let alone win an Oscar for it. But in fact, she did both.

Confidence is not a skill that has to be developed over time either. Otherwise, how do we explain the multitude of rock 'n roll performers—with age ranges anywhere from the teens to the mid-fifties—enjoying a similar level of success in their careers? If confidence was a skill to be developed over time, then as a rule the older performers would have more confidence than the younger ones. Here again, there are too many exceptions.

CONFIDENCE UNVEILED

If confidence is neither a skill nor the result of experience, then what is this mysterious human attribute that has the power to make anybody who has it wildly successful and anybody who doesn't have it ineffectual and unfulfilled?

Confidence is a natural state of mind that we are born with. That's right! We are born confident and confidence stays with us until we begin acquiring limiting beliefs that chip away at it. Whenever we see very young children being interviewed on TV (before they learn to "fear" the camera and be shy), they are invariably very funny and a delight to watch. Most times they are actually more confident than the adults they're talking to, which is much of the reason we are drawn to watching kids on TV. They are fearless and charming. And their ability comes across without having, in most cases, any prior broadcasting "experience."

However, as we grow up, we begin to acquire or inherit beliefs that limit the circumstances where we can display confidence. As mentioned earlier, the main culprit is the societal belief that we can't express confidence until we have earned the "right amount" of experience. If we fall prey to this limiting belief (and, unfortunately, many of us do), then we start moving away from our natural state of confidence and into a state of doubt. We begin to think that before we can proceed with something that we have never attempted before, we have to have the right amount of knowledge, training, or skill to match some arbitrary standard. Even though we may already have a natural inclination or talent for achieving our goals without this "necessary" experience, the limiting beliefs that we have acquired over time make us lose the confidence required to try for them.

The main drawback with making confidence something we have to "earn" is that once we meet our self-imposed criteria, our confidence only lasts until we encounter a new challenge we haven't dealt with before. As soon as we are faced with this new obstacle, our limiting beliefs return to take away our hard-won confidence until we acquire even more experience. Because we still believe that experience breeds confidence, any new challenge fills us with fear. As a result, we end up living our lives on a roller-coaster of highs and lows of confidence that becomes very wearing and disempowering.

As we learned earlier in the chapter entitled *Our First and Second Invention*, we have the tendency to think that we have to learn new skills in order to move forward in life, when in fact what we have to do instead is to *un*learn what's slowing us down. The same is true for reclaiming our self-confidence. The best way to acquire more confidence in our lives is by *un*doing the beliefs that are stopping us from tapping into our natural source, instead of just getting additional experience. This doesn't imply that we should stop acquiring new knowledge and skills (for instance, by quitting school), since they can be of great benefit to us. However, what we shouldn't do is to make them a *prerequisite* for our confidence. Interestingly, once we reclaim our natural state of confidence by changing our beliefs about it, we'll discover that we are able to acquire the desired skills and knowledge much faster, since one of the side-benefits of self-confidence is that it speeds up our ability to learn.

Let's now take a more in-depth look at why we believe we need experience before we can have confidence. Most of us have grown up with the societal belief that we have to be better than others in order to be successful. Since we want to live useful lives and contribute to society in our own way, we go to school to study and then specialize in a given field or trade. We also want our contribution to be special and different from everybody else's; in other words, we want to be unique by doing something that is "better" than what others do.

But there are a lot of us to go around, so we embark on a quest to compete against the world (the proverbial rat race). Since we believe that we have to be "better" in order to be unique, we conclude that we have to have more experience than everybody else. We end up working very hard so that no one can beat us and we can remain on top. We are constantly trying to hold off the competitors. However, when we realize that the process of being better than others may take an entire lifetime (after all, no matter how much experience we manage to acquire, there will always be someone somewhere who has managed to acquire even more than we have), we decide that we'll never have what it takes to achieve our dreams, or in other words, that we'll never reach the "right" level of confidence required. As a result, we give up and settle for less than what we are truly capable of.

But there's a flaw in the above line of thinking: "better" is <u>not</u> a prerequisite for "unique." Let's take The Beatles as an example. At the time, there were certainly better guitar players and singers than Paul McCartney and John Lennon. There were also better drummers than Ringo Starr and better bass players than George Harrison. They never were the "absolute best" at what they did, nor did they ever claim to be so. However, there was only one Paul McCartney, one John Lennon, one Ringo Starr, and one George Harrison in the world, and most definitely only one band called The Beatles, probably the most recognizable group of performers that has ever existed (in spite of the fact that the band has been split for over two and a half decades!)

Were we all duped by The Beatles? Not at all. They might not have been the "best" musicians and singers in the world ever, but what they were was truly "unique." Many other bands tried to copy the sound, the style, and even the haircuts in the vain attempt to replicate their success. But none of them were able to achieve the tremendous prominence of The Beatles. *The Beatles were successful because they had confidence in their own uniqueness and shared that uniqueness with the rest of the world.*

How "unique" or how special we are has little to do with our level of experience, but it has a lot to do with the fact that there is only one of each of us in the world. No matter what level of skill we attain, no matter how many other people exist out there that have the same or even a higher level of experience than we do, whatever it is they do will never be able to replace who we are because we are unique by nature. Our uniqueness is what makes us special to begin with, not how high we climb or how much money we make. Nobody can be better or worse than anybody else, as long as they honor their uniqueness. Those people who are perceived to be great at what they do are simply people who know how to tap into their own uniqueness more so than others.

A NEW SENSE OF FREEDOM

Confidence without preconditions gives us a renewed sense of personal freedom. When we are naturally confident, we develop a trust in ourselves based on who we are and not based on what we know or what status we have achieved in our lives. Knowledge and status may broadcast our uniqueness to the world, but they are not what "makes" us unique.

Albert Einstein is a wonderful example of self-generated confidence. In spite of his revolutionary achievements in the world of physics, he didn't rise from the ranks of the eminent physicists in Europe. The study of physics wasn't even a tradition in his family. When he was developing his early theories on the relativity of time and space, he was just a young clerk in the Swiss patent office in Bern working on his papers whenever he had free time. He didn't have a fancy office on a fancy university campus. As far as professional clout is concerned, he had very little, if any. But what Albert Einstein did have was a lot of confidence in his own potential. Even though his unique view of time and space was radically different than what anyone else knew to be true at the time, he trusted his instincts to bring his theories to life in spite of the lack of support from his contemporaries. Because of his confidence in his unique ability, he eventually managed to revolutionize the world of physics forever.

We don't *already* have to be the best in the world in order to "allow" ourselves to be confident. **We just have to recognize our uniqueness and accept ourselves for who we are instead of rejecting ourselves for who we are not.** In doing so, we'll once again begin tapping into the natural state of confidence we enjoyed when we were young children. It is this confidence that opens up our minds, our comprehension processes, and our thought processes. Confidence improves the efficiency with which our minds work, so that we can think better and faster and thus truly capitalize on what makes us unique.

Uniqueness is what makes our role models stand out. All of their titles and recognition are just by-products of a confident state of mind that is their (and our) birthright. In the end, confidence is how we win the game without even knowing the rules.

THE OPPOSITE RULES!

POPULAR RULE

Before we can achieve confidence in our lives we need to get the necessary experience.

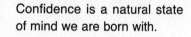

OPPOSITE RULE

Confidence is a natural state of mind we are born with.

PART THREE REVIEW

If you have uncovered one or two limiting beliefs about your career
or your achievements as a result of reading the chapters or doing the
experiments in Part 3, write them down below (we'll be using this
information later on in the book):

_____

_____

_____

_____

PART 4

REINVENTING YOUR LIFE

"Circumstances don't make us who we are;
they simply reflect our choices"

CHAPTER 4.1

EVOLUTION VS. REVOLUTION

So far we have covered a lot of territory in our process of reinvention. In Part 1, we began our journey by learning how our mind works, and by looking at the impact that our beliefs have on the way we perceive the world around us. We continued in Parts 2 and 3 by looking at how our relationships and careers are influenced by our beliefs, and how these beliefs create patterns of behavior in our lives. In Part 4, *Reinventing Your Life*, we'll learn how to let go of beliefs that place limits on our growth as well as how to develop new empowering attitudes to help us achieve and sustain a life of fulfillment and purpose.

Now that we have become aware of many of the beliefs that are holding us back, we are in a good position to start releasing the hold they have on us. We truly have the power to turn our present lives, with all their associated limiting beliefs, into the empowered and limitless lives that we are all entitled to. Things such as success, confidence, fulfilling relationships, and happiness—often so hard to achieve because of the many conditions we impose on them—can become regular parts of our lives we can enjoy any time we choose to. Instead of waiting for some specific outcome to take place before we feel good about ourselves and our lives, we can now use the strategies we have learned throughout the book to help us enjoy the *process* that each of us experiences along the way. As we move into this final stage of our reinvention, our personal challenge is to consistently incorporate these strategies into our everyday lives so that they eventually become second nature.

A WORD TO THE WISE

The benefits of reinventing ourselves are endless and the positive impact they have on the quality of our lives is very powerful and lasting. Consequently, it may be very tempting to try to implement all of the changes we want to make at once. After all, if these improvements to our belief system make so much sense and are so beneficial to us, then why pace ourselves? We might as well change all of our limiting beliefs in one big swoop, in a sort of "mental revolution."

However, when it comes to dealing with beliefs, trying to implement a large number of changes at the same time is next to impossible. We have to remember that our belief system is the "Mission Control" of our lives; in other words, it is our mental nerve center. Each one of our beliefs, the empowering ones as well as the limiting ones, controls a different aspect of our lives. In some cases, they propel us to higher levels of achievement and fulfillment, while in others they stop us dead in our tracks. But in all cases, our beliefs are simply doing the job they were designed to do: *ensuring our survival in the world*. If we attempt to replace our limiting beliefs all at once, they'll simply do whatever it takes to maintain their position of control. They will certainly put up a good fight and the best tools they have to fight for their own survival are our own emotions.

Let's use an analogy to help us understand more clearly how our limiting beliefs can try to stall our efforts for change. Imagine our life being a company where we are the owner and where our beliefs are the managers that run it. In our company, there are two very different management styles. About half the managers are progressive. They are the risk-takers who focus on growing the company to new heights. These forward-thinking managers represent our empowering beliefs. The other half are the conservative managers. They are very averse to risk and their main preoccupation is to make sure that nobody "rocks the boat." These protective-thinking managers represent our limiting beliefs.

Overall, all managers are loyal and committed to the company, since they've been working for it for a very long time. However, the polarized nature of the two management styles is a constant source of conflict. Whenever the progressive managers bring in ideas in order to move the company in a new direction, the conservative managers shoot them down. They always make the same compelling argument that since the company doesn't have any experience in that new direction, the changes will seriously hurt it.

In the midst of this argument, we, as owners, try to decide which way to go. If we choose to side with the progressive managers because we too want to take the company in a new direction, we know that we are going to face major resistance from the conservative managers. After all, they comprise half of the management team. So we try to reason with them by explaining the merits of moving in the new direction and the benefits that we all stand to gain from it. But they remain immovable. Since we know we can't make lasting changes unless they are willing to let go of their rigid standpoint, we continue trying to reason with them, hoping they'll change their minds. Yet, they continue to fight the change. In spite of their stubbornness, we even decide to move ahead on some issues without their support. However, we discover with great disappointment that we can't effectively move forward when a full half of the company doesn't embrace our new strategy.

After repeatedly failing to change the course of the company, we get very tempted to fire the whole lot out of frustration; but we reconsider: if we decimate the management ranks, who then is going to run the company? Firing all these managers would only leave a huge void, thus making our company very vulnerable and unstable. Now we find ourselves in a predicament because while we don't want to hurt the company, living with the status quo will only make us resentful owners.

A better solution is to take a more gradual approach. Instead of shocking the company with massive firings, we attempt to talk to each conservative manager separately and explain that we want to take our company in a more productive direction. If the manager we are dealing with at the time still refuses to change his attitude to move in the new direction, then we simply tell him that we appreciate the contribution he has made to the company and thank him for it, but since he is unwilling to adjust to the new reality, we have no recourse but to let him go. Over a period of time, we have the same meeting with each of the conservative managers, explaining our vision for the company and telling each of them that if they refuse to change, they'll have to be let go. This process is unhurried so as to not disturb the normal functioning of the company.

Releasing conservative managers gradually ensures that our company experiences minimal disruption. Also, while the conservative managers are being let go one at a time, we are replacing them with progressive managers as we build the kind of management team we truly want. Even though we know that we are doing the best thing for our company, we should keep in mind that since our conservative managers were very loyal in the years they worked for us, we might find that we feel a bit sad at times. Letting go of old friends is not the easiest or happiest thing to do. However, by making changes gradually, we discover that the experience isn't as traumatic as we had feared. Instead, this approach gives us the opportunity to adjust ourselves better to the new dynamics we are bringing into the company.

LIFE IS AN EVOLUTION

If in spite of our best efforts, our life is not getting to the point where we want it to be, there's a good chance that we have certain beliefs that are preventing us from getting there. As shown in the above analogy, in order to start moving in the direction we want, we have to replace those limiting beliefs that constantly remind us why we *can't* get there with empowering beliefs that constantly remind us why we *can*. But we have to make this a gradual process. If we want to change beliefs that do not serve us, then we have to do it in a way that doesn't shock our belief system. Otherwise, our built-in survival mechanism will kick in and make every attempt to stop us.

In order to make our change successful, we have to go through an "evolution," not a "revolution." We have to *evolve* those limiting rules of survival into empowering ones. We have to take our time, dealing with each limiting belief on its own. As our belief system slowly adjusts to our new empowering reality, we will be quietly changing our survival mechanism so that fewer and fewer things become threatening to us and more and more things enhance our enjoyment of life.

The next chapter, *Getting Ourselves Out of Our Own Way*, shows us a practical technique for letting go of our limiting beliefs in a gradual and nonthreatening way. Once we start replacing our limiting rules of survival with empowering ones, we'll be amazed at how much more daring we become and how much easier and faster we can achieve things that used to take us a lot of time and effort.

THE OPPOSITE RULES!

POPULAR RULE

The most effective way to make changes in our lives is by making them in one big swoop.

OPPOSITE RULE

A gradual approach to change is much more effective and lasting because it doesn't threaten our belief system.

EXPERIMENT
BREAK!

CHAPTER 4.2
GETTING OURSELVES OUT OF OUR OWN WAY

Our personal and professional growth depends as much on *undoing* what is holding us back as it does on acquiring new knowledge. In order to experience lasting growth in our lives, we must let go of those beliefs that place restrictions on our ability to achieve, otherwise we won't be able to effectively translate our knowledge into accomplishments.

The process of letting go is a key step in our journey of reinvention and it is the main topic of this chapter. In fact, all of the chapters up until now have been preparing us to get to this very point because it is here that we will learn how to release the limiting beliefs that we have identified so far. Once we get ourselves "out of our own way," we'll be free to embrace our path of growth unhindered by self-imposed barriers.

THE PROCESS OF LETTING GO

The process of letting go involves taking a limiting belief we have already identified and then releasing it from our subconscious so that it is no longer able to restrict our progress. It encompasses the following four steps: *Awareness, Acceptance, Readiness,* and *Release.* These steps build on each other and must be followed in sequence for the process of letting go to work effectively.

FIRST STEP: AWARENESS

The first step in the process of letting go is *Awareness*. It involves identifying and acknowledging our limiting beliefs. This step is critical because we can't let go of something that we are not aware of, or that we deny exists. For this reason, most of the contents of Parts 1, 2, and 3 and most of the experiments in the book were specifically designed to help us become aware of our limiting beliefs.

When we start uncovering these beliefs, however, it's possible that we will come up against some that are too painful to acknowledge. We may react by trying to forget about them or by putting them into the "I can't deal with that now" pile. If this happens, there is nothing to worry about. Wanting to put something aside is a normal reaction, since our awareness of this particular belief might evoke painful and anxious feelings. Just *acknowledging* that we have these feelings is a step in the right direction.

Incidentally, deciding to put a painful belief aside *doesn't mean that we have failed in our process of reinvention*. It only means that we may not be completely ready to fully examine and let go of this particular belief right now. Whenever we are ready in the future, we'll instinctively know it because our painful and anxious feelings will begin to subside as we become more prepared to face our belief.

As well, the awareness of our limiting beliefs could seem overwhelming at times since we may begin to feel as if there are too many things that are "wrong" with us. If this happens, it's important to remember not to get down on ourselves just because we have so many beliefs to cope with. This situation becomes much easier to handle once we learn the next step in the process of letting go.

SECOND STEP: ACCEPTANCE

Becoming aware of a limiting belief that has been burdening us for many years may arouse a lot of negative feelings in us. For example, anger is almost always at the top of the list. We'll either be angry at ourselves for having fallen victim to such a belief, or we'll be angry at whomever we inherited our belief from, or both. Being angry is not wrong or unhealthy. After all, anger is a perfectly understandable feeling to have and we should honor it when it first comes to us. However, **remaining angry forever will not help us rid ourselves of our limiting belief.** The same applies to any other negative feelings that the awareness of our beliefs may arouse in us, such as frustration, bitterness, and resentment. If we hold onto these feelings forever, we won't be able to let go of our limiting beliefs. On the contrary, being in a negative state will only help perpetuate the limiting beliefs in our lives, as this state will act as a constant reminder of how much they have hurt us.

Before we can let go of our limiting beliefs, we have to make peace with them. Making peace means learning to accept our beliefs for what they are, and recognizing that having them in our lives does not make us any less of a person. Once we realize that having these beliefs doesn't mean that there's something wrong with us, we'll be able to let go of them more easily because we won't be tying our self-esteem to them anymore.

We'll know that we have achieved acceptance when we stop harboring negative feelings towards our limiting beliefs. If we still have these feelings, then we haven't fully accepted our beliefs yet. Now, we shouldn't worry if we are unable to make peace with all of our limiting beliefs at the same time. Some run deeper than others and they may take longer to heal. We don't have to change everything at once in order to move forward. The best approach is to begin with the limiting beliefs we feel we can accept right now and not worry about the ones we can't just yet.

THIRD STEP: READINESS

Once we have become aware of a limiting belief and have learned to accept it, we have to be *ready* to let it go from our lives. Being ready is more than just accepting that we have a limiting belief. It also entails *feeling comfortable* with the idea of letting it go; in other words, while we might feel a bit apprehensive about the process, we know deep inside that this is the right thing for us to do at this point in our lives. It is important to note that we will most likely feel some resistance to letting go of *any* limiting belief, but as long as our positive feelings about letting go are stronger than our negative ones, then we know that we are on the right track.

If, on the other hand, we find ourselves having trouble letting go of a limiting belief that we have already learned to accept, it is because we might not be *ready* to let go of it yet. Even though, for the most part, our limiting beliefs have caused us to feel emotional pain, we've gotten used to having them around; in other words, we have become "comfortable" in our discomfort. Perhaps we still prefer the comfort of a limiting belief that has been with us for a long time to the uncertainty of not having it around. This reaction is not unusual since, traditionally, our society tends to favor discomfort over uncertainty. Given the choice between having a limiting belief and having a void in its place, we are more likely to subconsciously choose to hold onto the limiting belief.

In order to achieve the peace of mind necessary to feel ready to let go of a limiting belief, we first need to honor our fears about uncertainty. If not having this belief inspires great discomfort in us, then, on some level, we are not ready to let go of it. We have to respect that fear, which is telling us we don't want to release it yet.

If we feel a deep resistance to changing a limiting belief, it's important not to get upset about it. It's best to let that particular belief be and simply start out with one that we feel more *ready* and *willing* to let go of right away. The more difficult beliefs will eventually come around. The process of letting go is like any other skill: the more we do it, the easier it gets. Letting go of the easier (less threatening) limiting beliefs first will give us the courage and confidence to tackle the harder ones later because we'll already have a few successes behind us.

FOURTH STEP: RELEASE

In this fourth and final step in the process of letting go, we'll learn how to finally remove from our subconscious those unwanted beliefs that are holding us back.

This step must be done very gently, since we'll be letting go of something that has shared our lives for so many years. As a result of our common history, the process of releasing may evoke a range of emotions. The nature of these emotions will depend on how deep the conditioning of our beliefs is and how much our beliefs have affected us throughout our lives.

It is important, however, not to be afraid of becoming emotional. This is a natural reaction to a process that deals with the core of our emotions: our beliefs. It is *equally* important not to block our emotions when they do manifest. They are a sign that the process is working and they indicate that we are finally letting go of a limiting belief.

This last step of the letting go process may prove a bit more difficult for those of us who believe that becoming emotional is a sign of weakness of character. Unfortunately, releasing our limiting beliefs cannot be a strictly intellectual process. If we attempt to let go of beliefs using only our intellect, we'll discover later on that we haven't actually released anything (as much as we may want to think that we have) and that our limiting beliefs are still lurking around. On the contrary, fully expressing our emotions when they want to "come out" is a sign of strength of character because it demonstrates that we are trusting ourselves. As well, expressing our emotions reflects an honesty about who we really are.

THE FAREWELL

It is not easy to say good-bye to a departing friend because it always feels like a part of us is leaving with them. It's as if we are saying good-bye to all the common experiences we have shared together —the good times, the bad times, the laughter, the tears. For example, a few years ago a good friend of mine was transferred overseas by the company we were both working for and the people at the office threw him a farewell party on his last day of work. As everybody approached him to say good-bye and wish him well, I simply stood beside him waiting. We just couldn't face that awkward moment when we would have to say good-bye to each other. After everybody had left, we hung around reminiscing about the past experiences we had shared over the years, but still couldn't part.

After a while, it was time for me to go for my evening workout. Since we both used to frequent the same gym, my friend decided to come with me to say good-bye to his weight-room buddies. I still hung around as he was saying good-bye to everybody. Eventually, it was time for him to go home to prepare for his big trip. We both knew we couldn't delay the moment any longer, so we just looked at each other as if to say "You know, we have to do this at some point" and without exchanging another word, we gave each other a bear hug. Then I wished him the best of luck and he left. After everything was said and done, it had taken us almost three hours to get to the point of saying good-bye to each other!

Letting go of a limiting belief is akin to saying farewell to an old friend when life has decided to take us on different paths. It may hurt to go in different ways, but we know deep inside that we *must* move on with our lives, since preventing the two paths from going their course would only hold us back from our own plans and dreams.

An excellent technique to let go of our beliefs which fully captures the farewell nature of this process is the "Good-bye letter to our limiting beliefs." This is a simple technique that can be used to let go of beliefs in private or with the help of a friend, and just involves a pen, a piece of paper, and a few minutes of your time.

The technique (explained in detail in the experiment at the end of this chapter) consists of writing a farewell letter to our limiting belief as if we were writing to an old friend of ours. By humanizing our belief, we can experience a more effective closure than if we treat it as an abstract entity. In this letter, we tell our belief how much we appreciate him for having brought us safely to where we are right now and that we are grateful for having helped us become who we are. Then, we tell him that we have decided to move on in our lives and that we don't need him any longer. Finally, we thank him for his help in the past and tell him that we are now going to let him go. We end the letter with a simple "Good-bye, my friend."

A SUCCESS STORY

I first put this technique into practice at a seminar I attended several years ago. Our class had been split into small groups with the goal of helping one of the group participants tackle a problem in his or her life. We had about half an hour for the exercise, which would be followed by a discussion of our experience with the rest of the class. The woman we were helping related the following problem: at home, she had always felt taken for granted by her parents and siblings. Whenever she came up with an idea, everybody would automatically discount it as being unimportant. As a result, she felt she couldn't assert herself in front of her family. She hated the situation, but felt powerless to do anything about it.

One of the tasks we had to accomplish in our group was to help her identify any limiting beliefs that might have put her in this situation at home. In order to try to pin down her belief, we started out with the traditional intellectual approach. After doing some brainstorming, she concluded that the main limiting belief behind her predicament was the following: "In order to be loved I have to be a victim."

Seeing as the intellectual approach was so effective in helping her identify this belief, we decided to continue using the same approach to help her let go of it. After about fifteen minutes, however, we realized that we were going in circles and she was nowhere near a solution to her problem. So, with about ten minutes left for the exercise, I suggested that we use the farewell letter technique I had developed instead. Everyone agreed to try it. I quickly wrote the letter in my notepad, gave it to the woman, and asked her if she wouldn't mind reading it back to the rest of us.

She was very intrigued by the approach and was very keen to give it a try. As she started reading the letter, tears began to well up in her eyes. About a third of the way through, she was so choked up she couldn't talk anymore. For the first time ever, she was releasing a profound limiting belief that had haunted her for her entire life. We encouraged her to read on, and eventually she managed to whisper through to the end of the letter as we held her hands in support.

After this experience and until the end of the seminar, this woman went through the most amazing transformation. She literally became a new person. While before the exercise she had been quiet and reserved, after it, she became assertive and outgoing. Since she now felt she could finally be true to herself, she decided to adopt a new nickname: True! To this day, whenever I receive an email from her, she still signs her name as "True."

Since this experience, I've tried the good-bye letter technique with many other people and the results have been consistently remarkable. I strongly encourage you to use it to let go of the limiting beliefs in your life. This technique is very gentle and allows you to be in control of the entire process. Even though the farewell letter can be read in private, I recommend that you read it in the company of somebody who is a good listener and who supports your personal growth. This person can be a close friend, a supportive spouse, a supportive relative, and so on. In all cases, make sure you read the letter aloud. Doing it in silence is not as effective.

If this technique doesn't trigger an emotional response (that is, you remain intellectual through the entire exercise), then it's probably because the belief you are trying to let go is not the root cause of your problems. You may have to dig a bit deeper to uncover the real issue. If you do get an emotional response, then you'll know you are on the right track. As this happens, remember not to block your emotions, even if you end up crying intensely for several minutes. Also make sure you read the letter to the very end, even if your voice is reduced to a whisper. This is very important in order to achieve closure with your limiting belief.

Having an emotional response is a key part of the process of letting go and is very healing for your psyche. By going through with it, you will allow yourself to properly mourn the departing belief. After you process all the emotion through your system, you will likely feel as if a heavy burden has been lifted from your shoulders. Sometimes, you might experience a slight headache after you are done. This is quite normal and is the result of the emotional experience you have just been through. But don't worry about it since it'll fade away within minutes.

It is important to note that there's nothing in this process that can harm you in any way, since you are always in control of what happens. If, however, you find the process a bit intimidating, leave it for now and come back to it later. Don't force yourself to do it if you don't feel ready. Also, some people may prefer the more conventional types of psychotherapy to deal with their beliefs. This is fine too. The important thing is to let go of what's holding us back so that we can freely move forward in our lives.

Now that we have learned how to let go of our limiting beliefs, we are at a good point to start laying the foundation for making happiness and fulfillment a natural everyday occurrence in our lives. Starting with the next chapter, we are going to introduce empowering life habits that will take us a long way towards this goal.

EXPERIMENT:
THE PROCESS OF LETTING GO

This experiment takes you step-by-step through the process of letting go of your limiting beliefs. This is a gentle process that should never be forced. It's helpful to go through steps 1-3 on your own first and then engage the help of a supportive friend for step 4. Don't try to let go of more than one belief in a session—do only one at a time for this exercise. Remember, a gradual approach is the best one for our sense of security.

- **First Step:** *Awareness*

  Choose one of the limiting beliefs you want to let go of (use the reviews at the end of Parts 1, 2, and 3). Write it below:

  _____

  _____

  _____

- **Second Step:** *Acceptance*

  Write down any feelings you have about this belief (e.g. anger, frustration, bitterness, resentment):

  _____

  _____

  Why do you feel this way?

  _____

  _____

  _____

  Do you feel you can accept your belief for what it is at this point? If you can't (meaning you still feel strong negative emotions), then you should leave the experiment and return when you feel more at peace with it.

- **Third Step:** *Readiness*

  Are you willing to attempt releasing this limiting belief? List any lingering feelings or fears about letting it go:

  _____

  _____

  If you feel ready to change because your fears are not too strong, then you are ready to move on to the next step.

- **Fourth Step:** *Releasing*

  Are you prepared to allow yourself to express emotion? List any fears you may have about it:

  _____

  _____

  The "Good-bye Letter": Here is the letter to help you release your limiting belief. On the first line, rewrite the limiting belief. Then, read it out loud, preferably with the support of a friend. Try to be open to the experience. Let whatever happens happen, even if nothing does, because you can always try again.

  "I know that _____
  (the belief), but I want to let you know that I truly love you for having brought me safely to where I am now. I'm truly grateful to you for helping me be the beautiful person that I am now, but I have decided that I'm moving on in my life and I don't need you any longer. I would like to thank you from the bottom of my heart for your help in the past. But I'm going to let you go now. Good-bye, my friend."

  Some examples of how to begin the letter:

  "I know I am loved only if I'm a victim, but I..."
  "I know that if I'm not successful, I am nothing, but I..."
  "I know that I can't change because I've tried and failed before, but I..."

- Have you experienced emotional release? _____

If you have, wonderful! You've mourned a belief that's been holding you back (a clear indication of letting go). Now, think about the empowering belief you want to have in its place and write it below:

_____

If you haven't become emotional (that is, you've remained intellectual through the entire exercise), don't worry about it. It could mean that the limiting belief you're trying to let go is not at the root of your problems. Dig deeper and try again.

CHAPTER 4.3
ADDING PURPOSE TO OUR LIVES

Statistical figures in the U.S. show that heart attacks and cancer rates among men soar in the first few years after the mandatory age of retirement. After age 65, the life expectancy of retired workers begins to drop quickly. Why does such a desirable life circumstance, which is normally associated with freedom and leisure, generate such undesirable statistic? What mysterious force is behind the rapid decline in the health of otherwise healthy people?

This phenomenon has a name. It is called "Early Retirement Death" and is attributed to the fact that the men who are mandated to retire feel that their purpose in life has been curtailed. Whereas before retirement, they considered themselves to be useful members of society, afterwards, they feel that since they have stopped contributing to society, they don't have a true purpose in life anymore.

The powerful message behind this perplexing statistic is that regardless of all the leisure time and freedom attained, *without purpose, people seem to start losing the motivation to live their lives*. By removing purpose from someone's life, leisure eventually turns into boredom and freedom eventually turns into depression.

At the other end of the spectrum, there have been many books written over the years attempting to explain what makes people become highly successful. There has always been a great thirst in society to figure out the "recipe" for success. But judging by the extensive range of variables attributed to the creation of success, there doesn't seem to be a simple recipe. What there is, however, is a pattern that consistently emerges from all these books: *Highly successful people are always very clear on their purpose in life.*

WHAT IS "PURPOSE"?

Purpose plays a key role in our lives. When we don't have one or we aren't clear about it, we become demotivated and dissatisfied. Conversely, when we have an inspiring purpose we become highly motivated and fulfilled. Given the powerful influence of our purpose on our level of motivation and success, it may seem as if we are dealing with some mighty force that is hard to comprehend. Surprisingly, this key force of life revolves around quite a simple concept:

Purpose is that which gives meaning to our lives.

Let's briefly expand on this definition. For centuries, people have been searching for the elusive "meaning of life" under the assumption that somewhere there is a universal "secret" that will make our lives automatically meaningful and fulfilling. They believe that if one could just learn this secret, then all of life's questions would be answered.

While pursuing this mystical secret is a very noble cause, I believe that there is a significant flaw in the approach. When we look for the mysterious "meaning of life" as the answer to all of life's problems, *we are putting the onus for their resolution outside of us*. In other words, we are placing the responsibility for our own fulfillment on something or someone else.

On the contrary, I share the view that the meaning of life is something that belongs to us. I believe that this meaning isn't a "secret" to be found elsewhere, *but is instead a choice to be exercised individually*. This choice reflects what **we** feel is meaningful to us. By choosing our own meaning in life, we are then taking full responsibility for our own fulfillment and happiness. There's an anonymous quote from eastern philosophy that summarizes this view very eloquently:

> *"The Meaning of Life is nothing but
> the meaning we give it ourselves."*

Our "purpose," therefore, is simply the choice or choices that we make in order to give meaning to our lives. These life choices can be anything we want them to be and are different for each one of us. For instance, we can choose to undertake flying instruction towards a commercial license because flying planes is meaningful to us, or we can choose to work in a day-care center because caring for children makes us happy. These choices reflect the purpose to be a pilot or a child-care worker and are simply based on the fact that these professions are "meaningful" to us.

In the end, we are always making choices in life and choosing our purpose is really no different. As a matter of fact, we have the power to change our purpose at will if it doesn't serve us any longer. For instance, if we work as a bank teller, but don't really enjoy working with money and numbers anymore, then we don't have to stick with this particular job. Even if it means going to night school to study something less "practical" but more rewarding, it will be infinitely more satisfying than remaining in a job we don't enjoy. There are no hard and fast rules that say that we have to keep doing something we don't like forever. Our lives will go on whether we do what we like or not. However, reinventing our purpose so that we are doing something we really enjoy will bring us closer to our own personal success.

It's important to remember that people don't become successful just because they happen to stumble across some lucky predestined purpose. People become successful because they consistently make choices throughout their lives that are meaningful to them and they stick to their chosen purpose until they get results. Once they achieve what they set out to do, they then choose a new purpose that either builds on their previous accomplishments or takes them in a new meaningful direction.

Ultimately, purpose is the force that gets us up and out of bed every morning. The more empowering our purpose, the more motivated we are and the more fulfilled our lives become. Conversely, the more limiting our purpose, the less motivated we are and the less fulfilling our lives turn out to be. In the end, the quality of our lives comes down to the quality of the choices we make.

PURPOSE AND VISION

While our purpose provides us with direction in our everyday lives, our vision provides us with the "big picture" for our entire life. A vision expresses what we feel we want to accomplish throughout our lifetime and is not a concrete goal that, once achieved, is in the past. A vision is the overall direction under which all purposes fall and reflects what is most important to us in life. How empowering our vision is determines how empowering the purposes that we choose are. Our life vision can be articulated in a simple statement. This statement doesn't say how we will achieve it, but it clarifies our intention. Some examples of vision statements are: to help others, to entertain others, to make money, to create things, to inspire people, and so on.

With just these few examples of vision, we can see that there are some that are inherently more inspiring than others. For example, wanting to create things or help others is much more satisfying than making money just for the sake of it. Even if we have all the money in the world, it won't necessarily guarantee that we'll have a fulfilling life, *unless the money is the result of another more empowering vision*. In general, if the vision we choose helps us improve the world around us in any way (no matter how small our contribution), then it is an empowering vision.

> *How satisfying our lives are depends on how empowering our choice of vision is.*

While the vision we have for our lives is not likely to change much over time, choosing our purpose shouldn't be a one-time-only job. Instead, our purpose should evolve over time, changing as we change ourselves. Moreover, it isn't a good idea to choose purposes so large in scope that we get overwhelmed by just thinking about them. The purposes we choose should be manageable and achievable. The idea is to make choices that we can implement in our daily experience with our present level of confidence and skill. If we make choices that are too difficult to carry out and well beyond our level of confidence, we will become easily demotivated. On the other hand, if we choose purposes that feel comfortable to us, we'll be able to focus on the task at hand instead of doubting whether we "have what it takes" to achieve them. Don't concern yourself with the level of "sophistication" of your purpose. As your confidence and skills evolve, so will your choices.

As an example, if our vision is to help people, some choices we may make over our lifetime might include: becoming a leader in summer camp; then volunteering in a residence for the elderly; then studying to become a doctor; and finally, working in a hospital. All of these choices take advantage of those aspects of our lives where we are confident and skilled and they evolve as we evolve ourselves.

While it may seem so far that our purpose only applies to our choice of careers, let's keep in mind that it applies equally to our everyday lives, including our relationships and our lifestyle choices. For instance, we are adding purpose to our daily routine when we: appreciate the little things our partner does for us, do something romantic with our partner, call our friends to see how they are doing, exercise regularly, plan fun things to do on weekends, have a balanced diet, walk the dog, and so on.

Finally, it's important <u>not</u> to discount choices that are down to earth and not necessarily spectacular. The point is to choose something that feels meaningful to us because it fulfills our overall vision. Just because we are choosing our purpose for now doesn't mean that it must feel magical and ethereal. There is no magic involved in choosing our purpose. **The magic takes place when we put our purpose into action.**

CHOOSING OUR PURPOSE

There are no restrictions as to what kind of purpose we can choose for our lives and there is no rating of purposes from best to worst. All purposes are good, as long as they give meaning to our lives. What's important is that our choices be empowering and that they motivate us. We shouldn't worry whether these choices are going to work for us or not. If we believe in them, then it's just a matter of time before they produce the results we want. Also, we shouldn't worry about what other people will think about our choices. Remember that we are making them in order to give meaning to *our* lives, not to someone else's. If our choices serve us, if they support us, if they empower us, then all we need to do is to go ahead and enjoy the ride!

When it comes to choosing our purpose, we are faced with innumerable options. To make the selection process easier, there are three basic steps we can follow to guarantee that the purposes we choose make our lives consistently fulfilling.

FIRST STEP:
MAKE CHOICES THAT CAPITALIZE ON YOUR STRENGTHS

Of all the choices available to us, it helps to select a purpose that takes advantage of our strengths. Even if right now our strengths don't fully go in the direction of our overall vision, it's better to make a choice that capitalizes on what we are good at but that isn't 100% aligned with our vision, than to choose something that we think can take us more directly to our destination, but that falls in an area of weakness.

For instance, let's say that we want to run for public office since our vision is to help our community, but we become paralyzed with stage fright whenever we are standing in front of an audience. One possible solution to this dilemma is to use our strength in, say, book-keeping, and get involved with a community theater company where we can handle the theater finances. Because we are in an environment that supports public speaking (in an artistic, if not political, way), we can start building our confidence level by gradually taking on small acting roles in order to get used to being in front of an audience. While we feel purposeful and confident as we are helping balance the books for the company, we are also learning to over-come our stage fright. Eventually, we'll be confident enough to start moving more directly towards our political aspirations.

Making choices that capitalize on our strengths builds our level of confidence.

Oftentimes we get demoralized because we choose a purpose in an area of our lives where we have weaknesses, without realizing that we have strengths elsewhere that can help us easily overcome them. As shown in the above example, all it really takes is to be a bit creative!

SECOND STEP:
BELIEVE IT IS POSSIBLE

To guarantee that we find a fulfilling purpose for ourselves, we have to believe that our purpose is *possible* to achieve. If we choose to do something that deep inside we don't believe can be done, then even if we are very excited at the beginning, we will eventually become demotivated and abandon our purpose altogether.

"Believing" is the basis for achievement in all areas of our lives. What we don't believe is possible will never manifest in our lives because our minds cannot conceive of it. For instance, if we decide that our purpose is to create a company to market a great idea of ours, but we don't truly *believe* we'll ever get the necessary capital to get started, then no matter how good our idea may be chances are we'll eventually give up our dream. Since our mind doesn't believe it is possible to get the money we need, our actions will unfold to reflect this belief.

Before we can achieve our purpose,
we have to believe it is possible.

THIRD STEP:
TRUST YOU CAN DO IT

We have now chosen a purpose that takes advantage of our strengths and that we believe it is possible to achieve. Our last step is to trust that we can make it happen. In the same way that the second step was about believing in possibilities, this third and final step is about **believing in ourselves.**

For example, let's say Fiona has graduated from nursing school at the top of her class, but feels that a better purpose for her is to become a family doctor—for which she already has many of the strengths (step 1). She believes it's possible for people with her credentials to get accepted into medical school, and even knows of ex-nurses who practice family medicine (step 2). Now, there is nothing stopping Fiona from fulfilling her purpose <u>unless</u> she doesn't trust *she* can do it (step 3).

In theory, there's no reason why she couldn't get accepted into medical school because all the tools of the trade are there, the knowledge is in place, and her marks are excellent. However, if her mind cannot conceive of *her* becoming a doctor, then her actions will unfold to reflect this limiting belief. For instance, she may procrastinate in filling out the application forms and hence miss the deadline, or she may fail the entrance exam because she is overcome by the fear of being accepted.

We have to believe it is possible
FOR US to achieve our purpose.

Believing in ourselves and trusting that we can do what we have set out to do is critical to the fulfillment of our purpose. By allowing our self-confidence to reign over our fears, we can pursue the purposes in our lives knowing that we are doing the best we can to fulfill our vision.

Once we implement the above three steps, **there is no stopping to what we can do.** It's important to remember not to get discouraged if we have a setback here and there. As long as we are making empowering choices towards our vision, we are already giving meaning to our lives.

A SENSE OF PURPOSE

Purpose is simply reflected in the actions we choose to take every day. Having a sense of purpose means choosing to do the things we like *now*. Adding purpose happens in the present, not something we dream about for the future. Over a lifetime, all the purposes we do add up to a life lived with meaning or a life lived with regret. We can each choose to do something today that is meaningful for us, anything from signing up for a class to giving a long-lost friend a call. It's strictly up to us to decide what's meaningful and choose to do something about it. If we do so consistently, we'll have the guarantee of a long and productive life ahead of us.

Here's a wonderful example of someone living her life on purpose: Leila Denmark, M.D., is America's oldest practicing physician. She turned one hundred years old in February of 1998 and still has her office filled with patients up to ten hours a day, six days a week. She says the secret for her long life is that "I eat vegetables and protein at every meal, and I love what I'm doing." While she considered retiring from medicine in 1990 when her husband passed away, she reconsidered, saying, "When I can't see or think well, I'll quit.... And when I go, I hope it will be right here in this office."

THE OPPOSITE RULES!

POPULAR RULE

If somebody told us what the "meaning of life" was, it would be so much easier to have a fulfilling and rewarding existence.

➡

OPPOSITE RULE

Nobody can really tell us what the meaning of our *own* life is, except ourselves.

EXPERIMENT:
FINDING YOUR PURPOSE

The goal of this experiment is to try to find out what's meaningful in your life so that you can choose your purpose. Knowing your purpose will help you make the choices necessary to make your life more fulfilling. This experiment can be revisited periodically, as it sometimes takes a few tries to figure out what makes us happy.

- Write four purposes you already do on a regular basis (e.g. jog 3x a week, tell your partner you appreciate them, your present occupation, etc.):

  1 _____   2 _____

  3 _____   4 _____

These actions reflect your assertion that these things are meaningful to you in some way. You're already succeeding.

- Write three "impossible" dreams. Anything you would really like to be doing right now if your world was perfect. (running your own construction company, decorating homes, sculpting, etc.)

  1 _____

  2 _____

  3 _____

These dreams indicate what is most meaningful to you. While it may seem as if they are impossible right now, it's important to be aware of them. Knowing what makes your life meaningful will help you make choices that are in line with your dreams.

- Write your reasons why you can't achieve your dreams. These are the limiting beliefs holding you back.

  1 _____

  _____

  2 _____

  _____

3 _____

_____

- Now write reasons why you <u>can</u> achieve your dreams. These are
  the empowering beliefs that will propel you forward.

1 _____

_____

2 _____

_____

3 _____

_____

A return to the experiment at the end of Chapter 4.2 will be
helpful to release any limiting beliefs that may be holding you
back from pursuing your dreams.

CHAPTER 4.4
A BALANCING ACT

Oftentimes, when we learn that something is good for us, we feel that unless we do it to an extreme we are not really going to benefit from it. Or when we find something we like a lot, we feel that unless we get it all the time we are not going to be satisfied. Or if we decide to go after something we really want, we feel that unless we go all out we are not going to get it. It appears that, for some reason, there is a marked tendency in our society to gravitate towards extremes. Whether we work too much, eat too much, exercise too much, or spend too much, we honestly feel that unless we take things to the extreme we are not going to get a real sense of fulfillment out of them.

Interestingly, when we go to extremes, we end up having quite a different experience than what we had originally anticipated. Eventually, we reach a point where we either start burning out, or we become dissatisfied, or our relationships get eroded. Our approach to fulfillment ends up backfiring on us because by going to extremes, we have caused our lives to get out of their natural state of balance. In other words, we become so focused on a certain aspect of our lives that we end up seriously neglecting other aspects which are equally necessary for our well-being.

For example, both activity and rest are necessary for our sense of balance and health. Activity allows us to exercise our minds and bodies, while rest allows us the downtime necessary to repair and become stronger. Since they complement each other, having a good balance between activity and rest helps us stay in top form. However, if we make ourselves busy twenty hours a day, then we have no choice but to take time away from our rest and relaxation. We overexert ourselves with activity without allowing enough time to recharge our batteries. If we keep this up, we'll eventually begin to develop health problems. We might be more susceptible to colds or feel tired a lot of the time. Has it ever happened to you that you get a cold *just after* finishing an intense and highly demanding project? These health problems are our mind and body's way of telling us that we have overdone it and that now we need to rest, thereby forcing an end to our imbalance.

Activity and rest are natural complements that require balance.

Our career and our family life complement each other as well. Our career typically nourishes us with food for the mind while our family life provides us with food for the heart and soul. However, if we start working late in the evenings and on weekends on a regular basis, then we have no choice but to neglect the relationships with our loved ones, since there are only so many hours in a day. Eventually, we will begin to lose our partner's support and our children's interest. After a while, if we don't take any action to correct the imbalance, then the correction will be forced onto us. Either our married life will become deadened or it will come to an end all together. The jolt of this situation will wake us up to the imbalance that we have created and painfully remind us of the isolation we feel inside. Because we will now have to put that much more energy into re-establishing trust and connection with our families, our career might end up being neglected as a consequence.

Even if we don't have a romantic partner right now, we still need to have a balance between spending time at work and having a social life. If we think that working hard non-stop at the expense of our social interactions will get us ahead in our careers faster, we'll eventually reach a point where we'll prematurely burn out and lose our drive. In the end, both our careers and our social life will suffer.

> *Career and relationships are also natural complements that require balance.*

When we artificially skew our natural balance in one direction or another, we place ourselves in our least resourceful state. Since we can only function in this state for so long before we "run out of gas," our built-in survival mechanism kicks in to force us back into balance before we can do irreversible damage to our physical and mental health.

WHY WE GO TO EXTREMES

The question is, if our natural balance is our most effective state, then why do we have the tendency to go to extremes whenever we want to achieve something?

We tend to gravitate towards extremes because we happen to live in a world that celebrates outcomes. We always have the expectation that we have to beat the latest record. We celebrate, admire, and want to emulate the people who go faster, further, or higher than ever before. They become our role models and their achievements become our beacon for excellence.

There is no question that great achievements are an important source of inspiration for us. However, looking <u>only</u> at the magnitude of an achievement (how extreme the results are) and not at the *nature of the process* that led to it creates the false perception that the only way to get excellent results is to pursue our goals in an extreme way. In other words, we assume that in order to achieve extreme results we have to be extreme in how we go about achieving them. What we fail to realize is that the magnitude of an achievement is not the result of how extreme we are in its pursuit, but is instead a consequence of the quality of the process that created it. The better the balance, the higher the quality.

By maintaining a natural balance between activity and rest, work and play, career and relationships, and so on, we become our most effective selves. When we pursue our goals with a sense of balance in our lives, we significantly increase the chances of achieving great results.

THE MEANING OF "BALANCE"

One of the main reasons we don't give the idea of balance its due attention is because of the images that the word *balance* typically conjures up in our society. Given our "extreme" conditioning, we are more likely to associate balance with *being in the middle*, or *being average*, or even *not standing out,* than with effectiveness and resourcefulness. Since our societal conditioning tells us that we have to go all-out in order to excel, then we cannot conceive of succeeding from a point of balance. We believe that if we are balanced we won't push as hard as we can, and therefore we will only achieve mediocre results.

However, what we don't realize is that having balance in our lives actually provides us with a *stronger* foundation for achievement than going to extremes. Let me explain this concept with a simple analogy. If we go for a drive and one of our tires is out of balance, our car will slowly begin to shake. The reason for the shaking is that the unbalanced tire is providing the car with uneven traction, which results in vibration. If we increase the speed significantly, there will be a point at which the unbalanced tire will begin to bounce on and off the road. If we increase the speed even more, the tire will start banging wildly on the pavement and will eventually blow up from the repeated heavy impacts.

As a result, the faster we drive the car, the more ineffective and weakened the out-of-balance tire becomes. When pushed to the limit, the tire endures permanent damage and has to be replaced altogether. Because the tire was unbalanced, it seriously affected the quality of the ride and threatened the overall "health" of the car. On the other hand, when all tires are balanced our car can go as fast as we want it to go and the ride is always smooth, no matter the speed.

The same is true for our lives. When we maintain our natural balance, we have a much stronger foundation for achievement than if we are out of balance. We are more effective because all aspects of our lives are in alignment. However, when we are out of balance we experience similar side effects as our car did in the above analogy. The quality of the "ride" in our lives is adversely affected and our overall health is threatened. The problem is that we can't replace ourselves like we can replace a tire. Once we cause damage to our health due to our prolonged imbalance, we are stuck with it for as long as it takes to heal.

One of the ways we can start to regain our natural balance is to *be aware of when we feel out of balance*. Perhaps we feel moody, or overtired, or stressed out, or out-of-synch with the world. These are clues that we can use as indications that we are going out of balance. Being in balance is a skill that we can develop over time. It's not a one-step process that once we achieve it, we are done with it. I personally believe that balance is one of the most fulfilling and rewarding aspects of our journey of reinvention.

REGAINING OUR NATURAL BALANCE

Here are four very effective guidelines that can go a long way to helping us regain balance in our lives. We can easily apply these guidelines to a host of different situations in our everyday lives with very powerful results.

FIRST GUIDELINE:
TAKE SMALL STEADY STEPS INSTEAD OF LARGE QUICK ONES

When we are used to taking things to extremes in our lives, it is very tempting to try to regain our natural balance by jumping to the other end of the scale. We figure that the two extremes will cancel each other out and we'll then become balanced. However, this approach doesn't bring us to a true balance, just to an imbalance in the opposite direction.

As an example, when I graduated from college and landed my first "real world" job, my eating habits went out of balance in a big way. Since that was the first time ever I was making any serious amount of money, I got spoiled. I decided that I didn't want to waste my time cooking for myself when there were so many take-out places nearby. I soon got into the habit of eating take-out food four to five times a week. After about two years of eating this way, I had gained over twenty pounds! I immediately panicked because I was in my prime dating years and I feared this excess weight would lower my chances of attracting women. I made the decision that I had to get back to normal at any cost. But "any cost" meant going to the other extreme in one large quick move.

As a result of my decision, I completely cut take-out food from my diet. But I didn't stop there. I also cut out all desserts, fried foods of any kind, candy of any kind, sugar, bread, and all meat products. I shunned anything that wasn't either a fruit, vegetable, rice or yogurt. Unfortunately, in the process I became a very difficult and inflexible person to be around. In my efforts to adhere to my strictest of requirements, I ended up driving people away. And all I was doing was trying to lose weight for the benefit of my social life!

It wasn't until I decided to move towards the middle ground that I became less strict with myself and my relationship with food. Instead of making a bold change as I did before, I chose a more gradual and relaxed approach. I allowed myself to order take-out food again, but only when I felt like it, and not five times a week because I was too lazy to cook. I also allowed myself to have snacks every now and then (previously banned from my diet), but not as a replacement for the main meals of the day. By going towards the middle ground in smaller steps, I was finally able to regain the natural balance I had enjoyed before going to extremes. Soon, my social life started flourishing again. It wasn't very long after I regained this natural balance in my life that I met the woman whom I would eventually marry.

In summary, taking one step at a time towards balance is the best antidote against going to extremes. When we go to extremes, we exacerbate the problem instead of resolving it. Remember, a personal "evolution" is much less traumatic than a personal "revolution." By making changes slowly but steadily, we significantly increase our chances of achieving and maintaining a natural balance in our lives.

SECOND GUIDELINE:
ADD VARIETY TO YOUR ROUTINE

Another very effective way to regain balance in our lives is by adding variety to our routine. While having a routine is important in giving us a sense of purpose and structure, adding variety helps keep us interested in what we choose to do and gives us greater perspective. The old adage "Variety is the spice of life" is a perfect reminder when we want more balance in our lives.

Whenever we find ourselves doing too much of the same thing, whatever it may be, we need to give ourselves permission to "break it up" by adding other things that balance out what we are doing. For instance, if we have jobs that are very sedentary, it's a good idea to break the day with a walk or a jog, a squash game, a quick workout, or just throwing some basketballs. Many places of work now have their own fitness facilities or have access to facilities nearby. If our jobs involve a lot of talking, then we can break it up with silence (for instance, by going for a walk in the park). If it involves thinking, then we can break it up by listening to some music we really enjoy or by reading the sports or entertainment section in the paper. If we have jobs that are very physical in nature with a lot of demand on our senses (as in construction work), finding an oasis of quiet where we can go relax for a few minutes every now and then will help us regain our balance. If we spend a lot of time in our house, then we have to build daily routines that take us outside at least once a day. We can go for a short walk or just run an errand or two.

Adding variety to our lives is one of the easiest and yet most effective ways to maintain balance in our lives because it prevents us from getting stuck on any one activity. Once we start allowing ourselves to introduce changes in our daily routine, we'll discover that we feel more centered, effective and fulfilled.

THIRD GUIDELINE:
MAKE YOUR CAREER A PART OF YOUR LIFE INSTEAD OF MAKING YOUR LIFE A PART OF YOUR CAREER

For those of us who are career-oriented, it's important to balance our careers with our lives outside of work. We may be very tempted to focus solely on planning our careers because we want to make sure that we can achieve our ambitious goals. But sometimes, our personal lives end up tagging along without much attention being given to them. The exclusive focus on our jobs usually causes a large imbalance in our lives, as we tend to overcommit at work for the purpose of advancing our careers at the expense of personal fulfillment with our loved ones. As a result, our lives end up looking career-heavy with a weak "life" focus since we don't spend enough energy on our families.

The best antidote for this situation is to choose to *make our careers a part of our lives,* instead of *making our lives a part of our careers.* In this way, we can achieve a natural balance without having our careers fall by the wayside. Instead of planning our career alone in the seclusion of our office, we can plan it together with our families. We can still have strong career wants, but now we can make sure that we are taking into consideration our families' wants as well. What this does is make them feel like partners in our decisions. For instance, if some of our career goals involve extensive travel in the next year or two, we can either make this decision by ourselves and allow our families to wonder why we are gone so much, or we can involve them from the very beginning explaining why this is a good move for our careers and asking them how they feel about it. Perhaps they can suggest ways to make use of the time when we are in town to "reconnect" with each family member in ways that are meaningful to us and them. In sharing our wants and listening to theirs, we can more effectively plan our lives and have our careers fit nicely within them.

Having a successful career and a fulfilling life are not mutually exclusive. Neither are work and play, nor rest and exercise. However, if a part of us still feels doubtful that we can achieve this level of balance in our lives, the next guideline is perhaps the most important one for us.

FOURTH GUIDELINE:
BEGIN TO SET BOUNDARIES IN YOUR LIFE

There are many instances in our lives when we allow external requests to take us away from our natural balance. For instance, many times we overcommit ourselves because we want to be as accommodating as we can. Whether it is at work, at home, with friends, or with relatives, we want to look good in other people's eyes. As a result, we often do things that we don't necessarily want to do in order to please them. While we mean well, when we spread ourselves too thin, we begin planting the seeds for a life of imbalance.

For example, Anna is a software designer working in the Research & Development department of a large hi-tech corporation. Right now she is involved in a very important project with a tight deadline. While she is working longer hours than she would like to, she really enjoys her job. However, since she is known at work as being very good at what she does, every few days somebody invariably asks her to help them fix this software bug here or make a small change to that program there.

Anna feels that she can't say no to these requests because she feels she has to preserve her image of being a "nice person." Also, she secretly enjoys knowing that she is the only one who can help them. However, Anna has gotten herself into a difficult situation: because of the many small requests she has committed to doing, she falls behind her main project. As a result, she is forced to work late every night and on weekends at home in order to catch up, which throws her life totally off balance. She has to cancel a weekend trip with her friends that she had been planning for months and stops exercising altogether. Her life becomes totally consumed with catching up on her work, all because she couldn't set boundaries with other people. If Anna keeps up this state of imbalance for a long time, she may start having health problems and begin to hate her job.

When we are forced to go out of balance by external circumstances, we find ourselves faced with double trouble. First, we don't want to let someone else down by not delivering on our commitment, no matter how excessive it may be. And second, we don't want to lose credibility by reneging on our word. When we don't set boundaries, we put ourselves into this pressure-filled predicament. If we continually do this, sooner or later other aspects of our lives will start forcing us to take notice of our imbalance. Perhaps we'll start gaining weight or develop health problems or we'll start driving people away from our lives.

How do we learn to set boundaries in our lives? **The simplest answer is to learn not to be afraid to say no.** *Just* because people ask doesn't mean we *have to* say yes. Otherwise, our time can rapidly get encroached upon. After all, what's the point of delivering on more commitments than we can handle if we have to take time away from our personal lives and from our sleep? Eventually, if we get seriously out of balance our health will begin to deteriorate, and without our health we won't be able to enjoy the fruits of our labor anyway.

Now, if we are truly afraid to say "no" to others, perhaps we have a limiting belief that needs to be looked at. For example, such a belief might be: "What other people think is more important than what I want." This could explain why saying "no" to others is very difficult for us. Letting go of this belief will help us muster the courage to start setting boundaries with others.

Ironically, setting boundaries with other people makes us become more resourceful at what we do. Since we are not doing things at the expense of our mental and physical health, we are in a better position to carry out what we do commit to doing with more efficiency and enjoyment because we are *only committing to what we know we can handle*. Keep in mind, however, that saying no right now doesn't mean saying no forever. It only means that we are taking a proactive attitude in order to maintain the balance we need to live healthy and fulfilling lives. By scheduling our commitments around our well-being, and not the other way around, we will be able to deliver better and faster results because we will be doing so from a source of strength instead of one of weakness.

We'll know we have achieved balance when we feel a sense of ease in our lives. We've all had days when everything seems to go "right" for us and when we feel like we are on top of the world. *These are the days when we are the most balanced.* We are doing what we choose to do and don't feel a lot of outside pressure to do something different. Some people refer to this state as "being in flow," as life seems to flow smoothly.

Once we start practicing being in balance more often by using the above four guidelines and our own personal common sense, we'll discover that we become more effective and more interested in what we do. We'll also discover that when we are balanced, we can more easily fulfill our chosen purpose in life.

THE OPPOSITE RULES!

POPULAR RULE		OPPOSITE RULE
In order to succeed we have to go "all out."	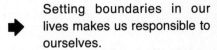	Being in balance helps us achieve a much more lasting success than going to extremes.
Setting boundaries in our lives makes us appear irresponsible to others.		Setting boundaries in our lives makes us responsible to ourselves.

EXPERIMENT:
ACHIEVING BALANCE

The goal of this experiment is to help you achieve balance in your life and to help you become more aware of when you are out of balance.

- Ask yourself how you can add more variety to your life.

  More work or less? _____

  More exercise or less?_____

  More social time or alone time? _____

- Think of two things you really want to do but never seem to find the time to do. List them below:

  1 _____

  2 _____

  Is there any external pressure stopping you from achieving them? If there is, ask yourself if you can say no to those pressures.

  Are you afraid to say "no"? If you are, why?

  _____

  _____

  Is there any internal pressure that stops you? What is it?

  _____

  _____

  What is the limiting belief that creates the internal pressure?

  _____

- Write below why you think that spending time on the above two things is worthwhile:

  1 _____

  2 _____

CHAPTER 4.5
THE PURSUIT OF (OUR ELUSIVE) HAPPINESS

If we ask different people what they want most in life and then ask *why* enough times, they will all eventually come up with the same answer: they want it because *it will make them happy*.

For instance, if we ask somebody what it is that he would most like to have in his life if money were no object, he might answer that he'd like to own a summer house in Hawaii. If we ask him *why* he wants a house in Hawaii, he may answer that he would eventually like to retire there. If we ask him *why* he would like to retire there, he may answer that he loves the all-year-round warm weather and the beautiful beaches. And if we ask him *why* he loves warm weather and beautiful beaches, he'll likely conclude that they make him feel really happy.

Whether we make it explicit or we disguise it with another intention, our search for happiness is ultimately at the core of our existence. We all want to be happy one way or another. The pursuit of happiness is even proclaimed in the United States Declaration of Independence as *a person's inalienable right*. In fact, our yearning for happiness exists equally in people of all ages. Whether we are three, twenty-eight, forty-two, or seventy-five years old, we are always striving for happiness. Of course, depending on our age, we may have different ideas about where to find it. For a young child, happiness may be found in his mother's smile; for somebody in her late twenties, in a meaningful relationship; for somebody in his forties, in a successful career; and for somebody in her seventies, in the love of her grandchildren.

What's very peculiar about this pursuit, however, is that as we grow up, it gradually becomes more and more difficult for us to experience happiness consistently in our lives. Somehow a number of "barriers to happiness" start showing up along the way of our pursuit. Some of these barriers are self-imposed while others are conditioned into us by society, but in all cases they inhibit our natural ability to experience happiness in our lives. Here are three of the most common barriers to happiness, as well as some strategies for overcoming them effectively.

BARRIER #1: RULES AND EXPECTATIONS

HAVING TO FULFILL CERTAIN RULES BEFORE WE CAN ALLOW
OURSELVES TO BE HAPPY IS THE FIRST BARRIER TO HAPPINESS

Young children know instinctively how to find happiness. They don't have a lot of rules they must follow before they can feel good. For them, the simplest of things can make them happy. For instance, friends of mine once told me that when they took their two-year-old son to the zoo for the first time, he was more enchanted with the ants on the ground than with all the exotic animals. Instead of being interested in the giraffes, elephants, and hippos, he was completely captivated by an anthill near the picnic area where they were having lunch. Their child was so delighted by these industrious ants marching in and out of their hole that he really didn't care to continue with the tour of the zoo. The little ants alone had totally made his day!

However, it seems that when we grow up we gradually begin to lose our ability to appreciate the simpler things in life. As we become adults, we start developing elaborate rules called "expectations." Suddenly, it's not that easy for us to achieve happiness anymore because our expectations spell out all the conditions that we need to meet *before* we can allow ourselves to be happy.

> *We allow our expectations to dictate*
> *when we can and cannot be happy.*

The most basic of our rules states that "I can only be happy if X happens," so we postpone our happiness until "X" is achieved. Usually "X" is something big and not easily attainable. No longer satisfied with little ants or the pleasure of a stroll in the park on a cool summer evening, we put our happiness on hold until we achieve some grand goal, such as landing the promotion we have been jockeying for, or winning the big contract for our company, or losing fifteen pounds by the summer.

According to these rules, we are *only* allowed to feel happy once we meet them. The downside is, of course, that we cannot allow ourselves to be happy *until* the rules are met. Consequently, we are forced to wait until we get that promotion, win that contract, or lose that excess weight to experience happiness in our lives. In a sense, happiness becomes the carrot dangling at the end of the stick in front of our faces that we can *only* get after we have met some self-imposed criteria. The result is that our happiness becomes hostage to our expectations.

As a matter of fact, not allowing ourselves to feel happy until we meet our expectations is one of the strongest barriers to happiness around. Fortunately, there is a very effective way to lift this barrier. All we have to do is to adopt the following strategy for opening ourselves to happiness.

OPENING #1: ENJOYING THE PROCESS

ENJOYING THE PROCESS OF ACHIEVING OUR GOALS IS THE FIRST OPENING TO HAPPINESS

By enjoying the "process" of achieving our goals and not delaying our enjoyment until their attainment, we begin to release ourselves from the hold that our expectations have on us. Instead of feeling tense or impatient as we are waiting to get results, we'll begin to have fun *doing what it takes to get us there*.

One of the best ways of learning to enjoy the process on a continual basis is to begin doing more of what we want and less of what we should. For example, if we are in a job we don't enjoy just because "we have to pay the bills," chances are we are not doing what we *want* but are instead doing what we *should*. Doing what we should isn't that enjoyable because it usually doesn't add much to our lives. Actually, most times it adds to somebody else's life at the expense of our own. Doing what we want, on the other hand, automatically gives rise to enjoyment because we are pursuing what's meaningful to us. Consequently, our life experience becomes more fulfilling, which in turn leads to happiness.

Keep in mind, however, that doing what we want does not imply that we should totally neglect the sometimes necessary chores in life. Eventually, we all have our share of laundry, mowing the lawn, or doing the dishes. However, we can still go for our wants by finding a balance between our desires and our chores. All we have to do is to "allow" ourselves to indulge in the little luxuries in life in addition to doing what needs to be done. This could entail spending a whole Sunday sitting in the garden reading a book, or going on a day trip every now and again. When we learn to do what we "want" more often instead of *always* doing what we "should," we will begin to get used to the idea of enjoying the process of achieving our goals. The result is that we'll experience happiness more frequently in our lives.

BARRIER #2: UNHAPPINESS AS A MOTIVATOR

USING UNHAPPINESS AS A MOTIVATOR FOR
ACHIEVEMENT IS THE SECOND BARRIER TO HAPPINESS

This barrier supports the belief that the only way to get things done is to be unhappy *until* they get done; in other words, to use pain as our incentive for achievement. When we use unhappiness as our motivator, we automatically make happiness the destination instead of the journey. As a result, we don't allow ourselves to be happy in the "process" of achieving our goal. The popular justification for this belief is that if we allowed ourselves to be happy all of the time, then we wouldn't feel motivated enough to try to achieve anything to begin with.

What we don't realize is that this threat of perpetual unhappiness causes us to waste a great deal of energy venting the feelings that come along with it, such as anxiety, anger, and frustration, instead of using our energy fully towards the achievement of our goals. We think, "Once I get this thing done, then I can relax." We put off feeling good until we feel that we have *earned* it. In the end, we hold our happiness hostage to the attainment of a far-off goal, without realizing that we are delaying the achievement of our very goals in the process.

Using unhappiness as a motivator to achieve our goals simply perpetuates our state of unhappiness.

A much more effective way of achieving our goals is to change our source of motivation to something more empowering than unhappiness. The next opening to happiness shows us a much better alternative.

OPENING #2: PURPOSE AS A MOTIVATOR

USING A SENSE OF PURPOSE AS OUR MOTIVATOR FOR ACHIEVEMENT IS THE SECOND OPENING TO HAPPINESS

When we feel purposeful in our lives, we don't need to motivate ourselves with unhappiness, since having a purpose is already one of the best motivators around. Having a purpose in life and experiencing happiness are closely tied together because when we do things that feel meaningful to us we automatically feel happy doing them. People who are purposeful light up when they talk about what they do. They find enjoyment and meaning in their chosen purpose and their pleasure is obvious to anyone they meet. When we have a purpose, we naturally enjoy the process. We don't need to put off our happiness until we achieve our goals.

Enjoying the process, however, doesn't imply that we shouldn't enjoy the attainment of a goal as well. On the contrary, celebrations are part of what makes life wonderful because they add variety to our lives, thereby giving ourselves a sense of balance. But when we live our lives with a clear purpose, we don't have to rely on the promise of a desired outcome to achieve happiness. While we enjoy the realization of a goal, it is not our only source of happiness; the success simply adds to the happiness we have already opened ourselves up to in our lives.

> *When we use purpose as our motivator, we are more open to experiencing happiness.*

Once we start developing our own purpose, we'll realize that happiness doesn't have to be a reward to be enjoyed sparingly, but can instead be a way of delighting in what is meaningful to us (if you're still unclear on how to find your our own purpose, you may want to return to the chapter entitled *Adding Purpose to Our Lives).*

BARRIER #3: HAPPINESS AS A REWARD

THE THIRD BARRIER TO OUR HAPPINESS IS THE BELIEF THAT HAPPINESS
IS ONLY A REWARD TO BE ENJOYED FOR BRIEF PERIODS OF TIME

Closely tied to Barrier #2, this barrier feeds on the belief that happiness is a temporary state to be enjoyed only as a reward for our efforts. When we use unhappiness as our incentive for achievement and happiness as the reward, we end up spending more time in a state of unhappiness than in a state of happiness. Why? Because in life we spend most of our time in the "process" of achieving an outcome, while the "outcome" itself is usually very brief.

Let's use an example to illustrate this point. Let's say that we are competing with thousands of people to be accepted at a very prestigious college. In order to get in, we have to pass difficult entrance exams that take months to prepare for and, on top of it, the competition is very stiff. We know that getting in will make us very happy, but in the meantime we feel anxious and stressed out (symptoms of unhappiness). We endure these negative feelings for several months as we study very hard, and finally the moment of truth arrives. The marks are processed and we find out that we've passed. We are in! Happiness overtakes us. We are thrilled as we run to tell everybody we know of our achievement and celebrate our moment of glory.

But then, the first semester begins and there are new challenges. In order to be invited back to the second semester, we have to attain a specific grade point average that is quite high. As we study to attain this grade, we are embarking on a new "process" towards our new goal. Since we don't know for sure if we'll make it, we feel anxious and stressed out like we did when we were trying to get into the school. These feelings stay with us until the end of the first semester. When we discover that we did indeed "make the grade," we are again ecstatic for a brief moment—that is until we begin the second semester and we discover that there are yet new challenges to overcome.

When our happiness is just a reward,
we end up spending most of the process
towards it in a state of unhappiness.

In essence, we end up spending a long period of time immersed in unhappiness in order to enjoy just a few moments of happiness, after which we return to another long period of unhappiness until the next goal is reached. If we continue with this pattern, we will have spent about 95% of our time in a state of unhappiness, and only 5% in a state of happiness by the time we will have lived our lives!

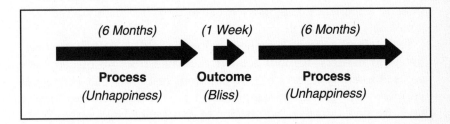

(6 Months)	*(1 Week)*	*(6 Months)*
Process	**Outcome**	**Process**
(Unhappiness)	*(Bliss)*	*(Unhappiness)*

If we learn to accept that happiness can be a state of mind instead of just being a reward to be enjoyed sporadically, we'll begin to have a richer and more fulfilling life experience. The third opening to happiness shows us how.

OPENING #3: HAPPINESS AS A NATURAL STATE

THE THIRD OPENING TO HAPPINESS IS THE BELIEF THAT
HAPPINESS IS A NATURAL STATE WE CAN ENJOY ANYTIME

As we have already seen, we tend to believe that happiness is a temporary reward to be enjoyed after we have endured a lot of hardship towards our goal. We also tend to impose a lot of expectations on ourselves and use unhappiness as a motivator for meeting them. While these barriers may proclaim that happiness is only a temporary feeling, the fact is that it's the barriers themselves that *trick us* into believing that our happiness is temporary. If we were to remove them, we would discover that **happiness is not a temporary state only to be had after achieving a goal, but is instead a natural state we can enjoy at all times.**

Happiness is truly in our nature. If we observe young children, we can see how simple it is for them to experience happiness. They find it so much easier to be happy on a regular basis because their list of rules isn't as long and complicated as ours, and they don't use unhappiness to motivate themselves. They enjoy anything that stimulates them, from funny faces, to shiny objects, to the flight of a butterfly.

Just watch young children learning to talk. They don't get down on themselves every time they mispronounce a word. They have somehow decided that their purpose is to learn how to talk and they keep trying until they achieve their goal. And they seem to be happy along the way. They enjoy their "process" of growth. Happiness is not some elusive reward they withhold until they learn how to talk properly. They don't need to fulfill a bunch of prerequisite rules in order to experience happiness because they feel happy already. It comes naturally to them.

This natural state of happiness belongs to us as well. If we bring down our barriers, we *will* achieve the same freedom of happiness we used to enjoy when we were children. Just think that even when we manage to block our happiness, it is still inside of us. In fact, when we give ourselves permission to experience happiness (say, by achieving a goal), all we are really doing is *temporarily* tapping into our existing natural state. Once we start removing these barriers, then instead of viewing happiness as a reward, we'll start viewing it as a state of mind.

When we realize that unhappiness does not serve us and that happiness is our natural birthright, then we can free up all of our energies and use them fully towards achieving our goals. Letting go of the above barriers—our rules and expectations, using unhappiness as a motivator, and using happiness as a reward—will make happiness available to us every day so that we can enjoy the process <u>and</u> celebrate our achievements, but this time without the crash back into unhappiness. In essence, we'll no longer be looking at happiness as just an end, but also as a *means* to an end.

THE OPPOSITE RULES!

POPULAR RULE		**OPPOSITE RULE**
We can't allow ourselves to be happy until our expectations are achieved.	➡	We can be consistently happy by simply enjoying the *process* of achievement.
Being unhappy is a good motivator for achievement.	➡	Being happy is an even better motivator.
Happiness is a reward to be enjoyed sporadically.	➡	Happiness is a natural state available to us all of the time.

EXPERIMENT:
THE PURSUIT OF YOUR HAPPINESS

The goal of this experiment is to open yourself up to your potential for happiness. We all have so many ways to be unhappy that it's time we balance them with new ways to be happy.

* Finish these sentences:

"I can only be happy if _____"

"I can only be happy when _____"

"I can only be happy if _____"

"I can only be happy when _____"

"I can only be happy if _____"

These are your rules and expectations for happiness (a disguise for our limiting beliefs). Here are some examples to help you get started:

"I can only be happy when . . .

        I feel there's nothing wrong with me."
        I lose 20 pounds."
        I'm the best salesperson on the team."
        everybody does as I say."

"I can only be happy if . . .

        people like me."
        I make more money."
        I find the woman/man of my dreams."
        I get a new job."

* If you've discovered limiting beliefs that are inhibiting your happiness, write them below. Try doing the letting go experiment at the end of Chapter 4.2.

_____

_____

- Write below sentences that reflect how you can attain happiness in your life without self-imposed conditions:

"I can be happy just by _____"

"I can be happy just by _____"

"I can be happy just by _____"

"I can be happy just by _____"

"I can be happy just by _____"

Here are some examples:

"I can be happy just by . . .
>   *being myself."*
>   *being with my partner."*
>   *reading a book."*
>   *cooking my favorite dish."*
>   *going for a walk in the park."*

- Think of simple ways to tap into your natural state of happiness every day (e.g. going on evening walks with your partner, reading to your kids, running every morning). List a few of them below:

_____

_____

_____

_____

Do two of these things this week and focus on simply enjoying the "process" of doing them.

CHAPTER 4.6
LIVING IN THE PRESENT

Most of us are creatures of tomorrow and yesterday. We manage to spend most of our waking hours with our minds focusing on what *will happen* or on what *has happened*. Sometimes we anticipate the future, sometimes we are apprehensive about it, some other times we worry about it. And when we are not thinking about the future, our minds are typically tuned into the past. We either have regrets about it, or we want to reminisce about aspects of it, or we feel the need to rehash it every now and then.

We believe that we have to focus on the future so that we know where we are headed, and that we need to remember the past in order to ensure that we don't make the same mistakes again. These beliefs make perfect sense, except for one very important detail we often seem to overlook: when our minds are so involved in the future and the past, *we neglect to experience the present*.

THE PAST AND THE FUTURE

Sometimes we have so many regrets from the past that we spend literally hours rehashing what might have been if we hadn't made the decisions we made, or what might have happened if we had said what we didn't have the courage to say. Some other times we keep going back to the past because on some level we believe that "things were better back then."

It's perfectly OK to reminisce every now and then about events that happened in our lives, *but not if we focus solely on the past at the exclusion of living in the present*. Maybe we feel angry about something that happened to us and feel unresolved about it. But we can't remain angry forever if we want to move on with our lives and truly begin living the moments we do have. After all, we can't go back in time.

While the past can be very helpful as a learning experience, we have to give ourselves permission to let go of the need to hold on to it. When we are able to let our past be, we'll be that much closer to enjoying the present—which is the only time frame we have any control over.

In the same way that we don't have control over the past, the future is equally out of our grasp. No one can accurately tell us what tomorrow will bring us. While we can make plans and have dreams for ourselves, we cannot dictate how our lives will unfold. That is in the hands of tomorrow.

When we constantly worry about the future, we do ourselves a disservice. We end up robbing ourselves of the very time we do have control over: *the present*. Sometimes, we focus so much in "what's going to happen" that we end up missing "what is happening." Here is a great quote I once read that made me think very deeply about my own habit of getting "stuck" in the future at the exclusion of fully enjoying the present:

First I was dying to finish high school and start college.

And then I was dying to finish college and start working.

And then I was dying to marry and have children.

And then I was dying for my children to grow old enough for school so I could return to work.

And then I was dying to retire.

And now, I am dying . . . and suddenly I realize I forgot to live.

— ANONYMOUS

If we are too focused on the future, then we never allow ourselves to enjoy what it is we were "dying" to get, even when we finally do get it. Our plans and dreams for the future, although very important for helping give our lives direction, cannot replace the authenticity of the actual moment when our lives take place. The only way to experience this authenticity is to be present in mind as much of our time as possible, otherwise we run the risk of *forgetting to live our lives*.

THE PRESENT

When we spend our time and energy haunted by the past or distracted by the future, we end up spending little or no time on what is the most fulfilling and immediate of all moments. The present is when things actually happen, when our lives actually take place. The past is always history and the future hasn't happened yet. But the present is what contains our genuine life experience. Obviously, it is in our best interest to learn how to live each moment more fully.

As an analogy, imagine that you finally go to see the movie everybody has been talking about, but instead of being "present" while you are watching it, you are preoccupied with thoughts about the important meeting you have to attend tomorrow, or you are rehashing the embarrassing situation that happened to you earlier today in the office. Chances are, you won't be able to fully experience the movie. While you are physically sitting in the theater, your mind is somewhere else. This is precisely what happens to us when we are not "present" in our own lives. Our minds are so often in a different time and space, that we end up missing our own "movie" of life.

Fortunately, learning how to be more present in our lives is easier than we think. All it takes is for us to make a conscious decision to truly "watch the movie." In other words, **we have to decide to give our lives our full and undivided attention.** By just "deciding" to be present, we can easily eliminate a great deal of future regrets. In fact, a good number of our regrets from the past are the result of not having been present at the time something important happened to us. Perhaps we were so concerned about the future that we didn't pay attention when a special "moment" happened. As a result, all we are left with is regret for missing it.

I'd like to share with you a story that my wife told me once about a friend of hers who forgot to live the present at a key point of her life. My wife's friend had been planning her wedding for almost ten months and had been dreaming about it ever since she was a young girl. She had planned every possible detail very carefully; however, she constantly worried that things wouldn't turn out "exactly" as she expected. Because she knew she only had this one day and that it was supposed to be "the most important day of her life," she wanted everything to be perfect: the flowers, the music, the dress. But whenever something wouldn't turn out exactly the way she wanted it (and, as in any major project, this is bound to happen a few times), she would become very frustrated and upset. So she ended up spending most of the planning stages of her wedding in a state of continuous stress.

Eventually, the day of her wedding came around. But she was still stressed out, trying to stay on top of every detail to prevent anything from going off track. As a result, she didn't allow herself to be really "present" on her wedding day. She was there physically, but her mind wasn't. Unfortunately, before she had realized it, the day had flown by. Her wedding had taken almost a year to plan, which she didn't fully enjoy because she was constantly stressed, and then the wedding day itself came and went and she didn't get to enjoy it either. *She was so worried about controlling the future that she never gave herself the time to enjoy the present.*

The sad irony is that this experience has since become her biggest regret! Because this young bride worried so much about the future being perfect, she wasn't able to be truly "present" for her own wedding, which created a deep feeling of regret about a past that can never be relived again. Even though she ended up with great wedding photos and a professionally-made video, in her mind, they will never make up for not having allowed herself to enjoy this experience *as it happened*.

THE CURSE OF PERFECTION

Oftentimes, we are so caught up in trying to make our lives "perfect" that we end up missing the process of getting there, like my wife's friend did. As we learned earlier in the book *(Fixing Our Procrastination Problem)*, trying to achieve perfection is the result of our fear of failure and it causes us to easily become overwhelmed by the details. Consequently, when we are trying to be perfect we are not giving ourselves the chance to relax and enjoy our lives as they unfold. Instead, we make ourselves slaves to our own expectations.

It's much more fulfilling to "let go" of our need for perfection, which keeps us locked in the uncertainty of the future, and instead "decide" to embrace the present however it unfolds. Once we are done with all the necessary planning, we have to let events take their course and allow ourselves to enjoy them as they happen. For example, when my wife and I were planning our wedding, we were astounded at the many details involved that seemed to steal our time away. But we also knew that we were planning a one-of-a-kind event that we wanted to enjoy. As we prepared for the big day, we promised each other that we would do our best not to worry about the details and to leave any problems that might arise on the day in the hands of our helpful friends. On our wedding day, it was challenging at times not to worry about events that were planned for later in the day, but we each made a concerted effort to "let it be." The result was that we both had a wonderful day. Of course, as with any event with lots of variables, there were some problems that did arise, but they didn't take us away from living the actual moments.

If we can learn to let go of our fear of failure and tell ourselves that we don't have to be perfect in order to achieve success in what we do, we can open ourselves up to being more present and, therefore, have more enjoyable lives.

THE MULTI-TASKING SYNDROME

Not only do we tend not to enjoy the big events in our lives because we are striving for perfection, but we also miss out on everyday pleasures that life brings due to our tendency to "multi-task." One of the main culprits for missing out on *living in the present* is that we are often doing several things at once. This habit not only reduces our level of pleasure, but in many instances also increases our level of stress.

How many times do we eat while watching TV, or use the cell phone while driving, or talk on the phone with a friend while making the grocery list? These are all examples of multi-tasking. In essence, we are not being fully present with any of the actions we are choosing to do. Since we are half-paying attention to each task instead of focusing on only one at a time, we are removing ourselves from putting in the necessary energy to be present. The result of our split-focus is either lowered enjoyment of our tasks, impoliteness to others, or even physical danger.

For example, cycling on busy city streets with headphones playing music increases our chances of being in an accident because we are not fully aware of the traffic around us. As well, people who drive while using their cell phones are distracted by their phone conversations which puts them at a greater risk for accidents. In addition to creating an unnecessary risk for others, both the cyclists with headphones and the drivers with cell phones also increase their own stress level because they are aware that they are not paying enough attention to their primary activity.

---

*Multi-tasking splits our focus
so we cannot be totally present.*

When we multi-task, not only do we put ourselves at risk and increase our level of stress, but also greatly reduce our enjoyment of everyday activities. Eating food while watching television is one such example. Since we are putting food into our mouths and not really paying attention to the taste because of the program we are watching, we are losing out on one of the simpler pleasures in life: eating. If we don't pay attention to what we are eating, how, then, can we monitor the quantities we eat? If we are watching TV, we are distracted; therefore, we can't really be aware of how full we feel. We'll more than likely finish everything on our plates even if we are no longer hungry because we won't be paying attention to the message from our bodies that we are full. If we are trying to lose weight, a great way to start is by eating and doing nothing else. Our bodies will tell us when we are full, but only when we are in a position to listen to them.

By starting to do things one at a time, we will greatly enhance our satisfaction in life because we'll be giving ourselves the chance to enjoy the everyday experiences that we so often fly by. Making a decision to be more present will ease the tendency to be "superman" or "superwoman" all the time, thereby curbing our urge to multi-task.

TAKING ACTION

In addition to enjoying our lives better, learning to be present holds an important key to fulfillment in our lives: *the power to take action*. The best plans we develop, the best ideas we come up with, and the best of intentions we have, won't be of much use to us unless we are able to turn them into action. Action is what turns our thoughts into reality. It's what allows us to give our lives the direction we want.

To paraphrase the age-old metaphor, life is like a river. If we navigate our river of life on a raft with no paddles, then we are at the mercy of the current. Wherever the current goes, we'll be taken with it, whether that is where we want to go or not. If we use the paddles, which represent our actions, *we* then become in charge of the direction our lives take us instead.

Bear in mind, however, that *actions can only take place in the present*. If our minds are preoccupied by worry about the future or consumed by regrets from the past, then it becomes very difficult for us to take action in our lives. Whether we are trying to make an important phone call, or start jogging in the morning, or look through the want ads, all of these things can only happen in the present, in the moment we decide to do them. If we want to change our purpose in life, our change begins with a single action that can only take place in the present. Yet, if our mind is "somewhere else," then it's highly unlikely that we'll ever make these things happen in our lives. Remember, there's always an ample supply of excuses available to us, but they are usually based on either the past or the future. Interestingly, in the present, there can be no excuses, only action.

LIVING IN THE PRESENT

All it really takes to be present is to simply *decide* to be so. However, since we are so used to thinking forward and backward in time, it's a good idea to first practice being present with simple tasks. This will help us slowly retrain our minds so that we start focusing on the "now." A good way to achieve this goal is by doing something every day that we really enjoy and by making a point of savoring the experience.

For instance, if you have a music album that you really enjoy, but that you hardly ever listen to anymore, make a point of listening to it and truly "getting into the music." In other words, not only listen to the music, but savor it. Try not to do any other activity that takes your mind away from it. Just sit down and relax, or dance to it if that's what you like to do, or if it's classical music you are listening to, play orchestra conductor. Do whatever allows you to give the music your full and undivided attention.

If you like going for daily walks, then make a point of "taking in" the scenery, even if all you see around are buildings and highways. Instead of covering your ears with headphones, experiment with listening to the sounds around you. Try also to entertain no other thoughts except those that are inspired by what comes into your field of vision. Maybe you'll notice architectural details you've never seen before, even though you might have walked by the same building every day for several years. Or you may want to observe the cars going about and focus on the different colors, designs, and makes.

If you are walking or jogging in the woods or in a park, pay attention to the different textures of the trees, plants, and flowers. Also, a neat experience is to listen carefully to the sounds of nature. You'll be surprised at how many different sounds are out there that we manage to completely block out with our busy thinking.

It is truly amazing how being present with simple things can bring about meaningful changes in our lives. For starters, you'll begin to enjoy aspects of your life that you might have taken for granted before. For instance, you may rediscover how beautiful your house really is, or how much you enjoy your favorite chair or couch, or how good it feels to hold a freshly opened newspaper in your hands when you are having your favorite drink in the morning. Yes, these *are* simple things, but we don't need a complicated challenge in order to learn to be present. In fact, the simple things are the best to practice on.

The following is a poem written by an eighty-five year old woman from Louisville, Kentucky by the name of Nadine Stair, in which she contemplates her own life experience and what she would do differently if she could live her life all over again. Her words wonderfully capture the importance of living in the present every day:

> If I had my life to live over again, I'd dare to make more mistakes next time. I'd relax. I'd limber up. I'd be sillier than I've been this trip. I would take fewer things seriously. I would take more chances, I would take more trips, I would climb more mountains and swim more rivers and I would watch more sunsets. I would eat more ice cream and fewer beans. I would, perhaps, have more actual troubles and fewer imaginary ones. You see, I was one of those people who lived sensibly and sanely, hour after hour, day after day.
>
> Oh, I've had my moments and if I had it to do over again, I'd have many more of them. In fact, I'd try to have nothing else—just moments, one after another, instead of living so many years ahead of each day. I've

been one of those persons who never goes anywhere without a thermometer, a hot-water bottle, a raincoat, and a parachute. If I had it to do all over again, I'd travel lighter than I have.

If I had my life to live over, I would start barefoot earlier in the spring and I'd stay that way later in the fall. I would go to more dances, I would ride more merry-go-rounds, I would pick more daisies.

— NADINE STAIR

Time has two very stubborn habits. First, it only runs in one direction: forward. And second, it never stops to wait for us. Living in the present is the best antidote for the passage of time because it allows us to seize the day every day and, thus, thoroughly enjoy our time on earth. From the smallest chores to our greatest accomplishments, there is no better experience than a life lived to the fullest. Like Nadine Stair, we only get one chance to live our lives. *We might as well enjoy it as it happens!*

THE OPPOSITE RULES!

POPULAR RULE		OPPOSITE RULE
If we don't think about the past, then we are bound to make the same mistakes again.	➡	If we **always** live in the past, then we rob ourselves from enjoying the present.
If we are not concerned about the future, then we won't have any control over it when it happens.	➡	If we constantly worry about the future, then we end up missing the only time we have full control over: *the present*.

EXPERIMENT:
LEARNING TO LIVE IN THE PRESENT

The goal of this experiment is to practice living each moment as it unfolds. We'll discover at first that inevitably we have thoughts from the past and thoughts about the future that invade our moments. Nevertheless, we can allow these thoughts to just come in and out as we learn to savor the present.

- List three regrets and three worries:

  "I regret that _____"

  "I regret that _____"

  "I regret that _____"

  "I worry that _____"

  "I worry that _____"

  "I worry that _____"

  These are some things that are keeping you locked in the past and the future instead of focused on the present.

- Name three things you really enjoy doing:

  1 _____

  2 _____

  3 _____

  Do each one this week.

- Make a point of practicing living the moments in your everyday life. e.g. try to listen more when others are talking and really hear what they're saying, pay attention when you're driving, really savor your meals, etc.

- Feel your life become much more fulfilling as you learn to truly live in the present.

PART 5

REINVENTING YOUR WORLD

*"The longest of journeys
begins with a single step"*

CHAPTER 5.1

MAKING A DIFFERENCE

Throughout the course of this book, we have uncovered many of the limiting beliefs that exist in our society and have learned how to identify many of our own. We have also looked at new empowering beliefs and attitudes that we can use in order to condition ourselves with a new "limitless" mindset. We now have the knowledge and the tools from our process of reinvention to slowly but permanently undo all the limited conditioning in our minds so that we can finally take charge of the direction we want our lives to have.

Now, how do we go about implementing all these changes in our lives? The success of our process of personal reinvention depends on two things: one, how effectively we let go of the limiting beliefs that prevent us from tapping into our full potential; and two, how effectively we adopt new empowering beliefs in their place. In both cases, the key to our success lies in **taking responsibility for our own reinvention.**

Taking responsibility means deciding to take charge of our own growth. It means taking initiative for making changes in our lives. It means accepting where we are and not blaming others for our "shortcomings." It means making firm decisions and sticking to them until we get results. Placing responsibility for our reinvention on someone or something else (like on this book, or any other book for that matter) won't make our changes happen, at least not in the long term. Ultimately, no one can change us but ourselves.

That said, keep in mind that taking responsibility doesn't mean tackling all of the problems at once. There is enough material in this book to keep you busy for a while. You don't have to achieve everything in the first week or even the first month. Change can take time. Sometimes, we may quickly get rid of a limiting belief, while other times we may have to try again and again. The deeper the belief is ingrained, the more work it may take to let go of. The key is to be patient with yourself and not expect to solve everything at once. Take comfort in knowing that most great accomplishments were achieved one step at a time. The same is true about making lasting changes in our lives.

Also, be very gentle with yourself. If you don't succeed right away, try not to get down on yourself. Letting go of a limiting belief can be quite a challenging experience. Be happy with the knowledge that you're doing your best given your present circumstances and you won't be disappointed.

OUR LIFE PATH

Through our process of personal reinvention, we have become aware of many of the beliefs that have been stalling our growth. As a result, it may be tempting to think that there are a lot of things that are wrong with us, that we have been doing the wrong thing, or that we have been in the wrong place at the wrong time.

But as we learned earlier, all the labels that we have become so fond of using to qualify things in our life experience—right and wrong, good and bad, and so on—are simply the result of our own perception. The fact is that no matter where we are in life, no matter what we do, and no matter how we choose to label our experience, each one of us is on our own unique life path. And as shocking as this may sound, **we are precisely where we should be.** This doesn't mean that we can't be somewhere else tomorrow; it simply means that there is a purpose for being where we are *right now*. In fact, the reason a lot of people are unhappy with themselves is that they live their lives believing that they are on the wrong path. Not surprisingly, people who are consistently happy are so because they have accepted the path they are on and believe that they are *just* where they should be.

Even in the face of a setback, we still have the option to accept the new direction our path has taken us and grow as a result, or to reject it outright and let time pass us by while pondering what our lives "could have been." Christopher Reeve is one courageous person who has fully accepted a totally unexpected change of direction in his life path and has moved on in his journey. The icon of superhuman strength in the 1980s, he was the quintessential Superman. An actor of great appeal and talent, he represented the ideal combination of manliness, strength, seeker of justice, and savior of humankind. In May 1995, he was riding his horse and had a serious fall. The accident damaged his spinal cord such that he was left a quadriplegic and had to use a machine to help him breathe. The accident sent shock waves throughout the world. How could Superman be rendered a quadriplegic? It was unfathomable.

After many months of recovery, he learned how to function in his new state. The emotional toll was great as he and his family struggled with the change this accident brought to their lives. Within a year, however, he founded a charitable organization called The Christopher Reeve Foundation which raises money for research into spinal cord injuries and made it his mission to find a way for all victims of these injuries to walk again.

Christopher Reeve didn't hide from the world. Although he had one of the most challenging experiences a person could have, he fully accepted his path and moved on with his life. He could've stayed at home locking the doors to reporters because he didn't want to be seen as anything less than Superman. But he didn't. He chose to believe something different about himself. He chose to embrace this new path in his life as the "right" path for him to be on and to use the opportunity to find a way to help others in similar circumstances.

His courage in the face of adversity is inspiring. If he can accept where he's at and still pursue his wants, do we really have a strong enough reason not to accept our own path, whatever it may be?

All we have to do is recognize and accept that *right now* we are on the path we need to be on and reject the temptation to believe that we are on the wrong one. If we ever stop growing in our lives, it's not because we are living on the wrong path; it's because we *believe* that we should be somewhere else. This belief causes us to spend a good part of our lives feeling unhappy. *It is our unhappiness that stunts our growth, not how "right" or "wrong" our path is!*

We will only allow ourselves to truly grow when we decide to accept and learn from our own life experience, no matter where we happen to be and no matter what we happen to be doing. Our decision to accept where we are will provide our path with the necessary bends and curves to aim it where we truly want it to go. In essence, before we can achieve our goals, we have to *believe* that we are on the right path for us.

Remember, whether we believe that we are on the right path or the wrong path, our mind will only see the one that we choose and it will shape our reality accordingly. So, given the alternative, *it only makes sense to choose to believe that we are always on the "right" path.*

IT'S NEVER TOO LATE

Do you think you are too old and that it's too late to be worth making any changes in your life? These are just limiting beliefs that you can change if you want to. Here are some great examples for encouragement:

John Mahoney emigrated to the United States from Manchester, England after high school. He then decided to go to college, where he graduated with a B.A. and then an M.A. in English. After moving through several jobs, as a hospital orderly, a medical-journal editor, and a college professor, he realized that none of them fulfilled him. So he made a 180° change of direction in his career. At age thirty seven, he decided to take up acting and enroll in classes at a theater in Chicago, where he was living at the time. After a while, he was invited to join a professional theater company. His dedicated work in this company led him eventually to receiving several Drama Desk nominations and a Tony Award. More recently, he has been portraying Martin Crane, Dr. Frasier Crane's ex-cop father, in the highly successful TV sitcom *Frasier*.

Betsey and Sam Farber decided to embrace their passion for cooking after they both retired from their regular jobs. However, an unexpected thorn came in the way of their retirement passion: they found ordinary kitchen gadgets very painful to operate. Most of the tools they were using made Betsey's arthritis flare up and Sam's hands sore. They looked around for kitchen tools that were more user-friendly, but couldn't find them anywhere. So they decided to create their own ergonomically-designed kitchen tools. Since they thought their tools could help other people who found themselves in a similar predicament, they decided to create a company to sell them.

Since then, their company, *OXO Good Grips,* has won several design awards from The Arthritis Foundation and the Industrial Designers Society of America. Now, it is an international company.

Anna Mary Robertson Moses was the housewife of a farmer in upstate New York for most of her life. At age sixty seven, she started painting as a hobby. After painting off and on for a few years, she decided to do it in earnest and began displaying her paintings in county fairs. She was then seventy-five years old. Three years later, she was discovered by an art collector from New York City and her paintings began to receive more and more exposure. In the years to follow, she became famous as her paintings began to gain notoriety. It wasn't long after that she got the nickname "Grandma Moses" and her work became an icon in American folk art. She continued to paint for the next two decades until very close to her death at age one hundred and one.

"I'm too old" or "It's too late" are nothing but limiting beliefs. Like any other beliefs, they are fully under our control and are totally replaceable. In the end, we are the ones who truly "run the show," as much as we are taught to believe the opposite. When it comes to making changes in our lives, we have the ultimate say. If we end up doing what others think we should, it's only because on some level *we* have made the decision to believe that their ideas are worthier than our own. If we want to change, we have to start believing in what *we* want to do, no matter what other people's "opinions" are. And we have to *believe* that the changes we want to make are worth it, regardless of our age or our circumstances.

Life consists of a collection of "moments." This very moment and every moment after it <u>are</u> what our lives are made of. If we live our lives worrying about the future, or regretting the past, or living how others tell us to live, then we are not living "our" moments. All it really takes to become in charge of our own lives is to simply decide to do so. Our process of reinvention is one hundred percent ours. Don't be afraid to use it fully to your advantage. Don't be afraid to think big thoughts. Remember, you *can* make a difference: you **are** the difference!

As the book now comes to a close, I would like to leave you with an excerpt from Marianne Williamson's book *A Return to Love* that was read by Nelson Mandela during his inauguration as president of South Africa in May 1994. These thoughts have been a great source of inspiration throughout my own process of reinvention. It's been a great pleasure sharing these pages with you and I wish you with all my heart the very best in your journey of self-discovery. Have a wonderful and happy life: you deserve it! ***Happy reinventing!***

Our deepest fear is not that we are inadequate.
Our deepest fear is that we are powerful beyond measure.
It is our light not our darkness that most frightens us.
We ask ourselves, who am I to be brilliant, gorgeous,
talented and fabulous?

Actually, who are you not to be?
You are a child of God.
Your playing small doesn't serve the world.
There's nothing enlightened about shrinking so that other
people won't feel insecure around you.
We were all meant to shine, as children do.
We were born to make manifest the glory of God that is
within us.

It's not just in some of us;
it's in everyone.
And as we let our own light shine, we unconsciously give
people permission to do the same.

As we are liberated from our own fear, our presence
automatically liberates others.

Experiment Index

INDEX

Do you know someone who could benefit from reading *How to Reinvent Yourself?*

If you would like us to send someone you love the gift of reinvention, or if you would like to receive additional copies yourself, please call our *reinvention line* toll free at:

1-888-830-8805

or

(416) 686-7949

local calls from the 416
and 905 area codes

You can also email your order to: *orderdesk@reinvention.net,* or fax it to: (416) 686-6716. Please make sure to include your name, address, telephone number, and time of day when you can be reached. For orders of ten or more books we offer a discount. Please allow 1-3 weeks for delivery.

SEMINARS

For information about Marcellus B. Andersen's seminars and public speaking engagements, please call our *reinvention line* at the numbers listed above, or visit us on the Internet at our Web site:

http://www.reinvention.net

We would love to hear about your experience with *How to Reinvent Yourself.* If you wish to drop us a line, you can send us an email at *comments@reinvention.net,* or you can write to us at the following address:

Brooke*Press*
2439 Eglinton Avenue East
P.O. Box 277, Station A,
Scarborough, Ontario
Canada M1K 5C1